BEARDED COLLIE
Bearded Collie Training

Think Like a Dog ~ But Don't Eat Your Poop!

Here's EXACTLY How to Train Your Bearded Collie

By Paul Allen Pearce

PAUL ALLEN PEARCE
P U B L I S H I N G

What Our Customers Say — About Their Results!

- ~ - ~ - ~ - ~ - - ~ - ~ - ~ - 5 Star Reviews - ~ - ~ - ~ - ~ - -- ~ - ~ - ~ -

5.0 out of 5 Stars! | Awesome!

"Awesome book! Great for my dog and I"

- Michelle Dexter

- ~ - ~ - ~ - ~ - - ~ - ~ - ~ - 5 Star Reviews - ~ - ~ - ~ - ~ - -- ~ - ~ - ~ -

5.0 out of 5 Stars! | Training!

"This book has helped me greatly. I recently adopted a 9 month old dog, named 'Ecko' after my dog passed away. I live in the country with a huge back yard and absolutely adore her. She is a wonderful addition." Thank you, Alison

-Alison

- ~ - ~ - ~ - ~ - - ~ - ~ - ~ - 5 Star Reviews - ~ - ~ - ~ - ~ - -- ~ - ~ - ~ -

5.0 out of 5 Stars! | Five Stars!

"Easy instructions, well organized, and fun to read!"

-Vicki Cisneros

- ~ - ~ - ~ - ~ - - ~ - ~ - ~ - 5 Star Reviews - ~ - ~ - ~ - ~ - -- ~ - ~ - ~-

5.0 out of 5 Stars! | Puppy Training With a Sense of humor!

"Not only was this an easy read, it was humorous. I realized that's the part I'm missing when training a pup - a sense of humor. All steps were clearly outlined in addition to what to do if the first attempts don't work out. This book was a great read and very helpful."

- Pamela Cozart

- ~ - ~ - ~ - ~ - - ~ - ~ - ~ - 5 Star Reviews - ~ - ~ - ~ - ~ - -- ~ - ~ - ~
-

5.0 out of 5 Stars! | Very Well Written & Entertaining

"Very well written and funny. Definitely speaks to the dog owner. The only problem I can see is possible 'operator error' lol."

-Jeanette Lucas

5.0 out of 5 Stars! | Murphy's Rules

"This is a very informative book and gets the message across in a funny comedic way while still being serious."

-K Pierce

5.0 out of 5 Stars! | How Brilliant This Is

"This is a no nonsense, straightforward instructional training guide for you dog. Any one who has ever had a puppy knows how brilliant dogs are. You need to understand how they think and react to kindness and challenges. A must for GSD but also an excellent guide for any dog owner."

- R. A. MOON

5.0 out of 5 Stars! | Excellent Resource of Information You Need To Know

"An excellent resource of information for to know my dog's history and for training him. It really works, and he teaches patience."

-Clarice B

- ~ - ~ - ~ - - - ~ - ~ - - 5 Star Reviews - ~ - ~ - ~ - ~ -- ~ - ~ - ~ -

5.0 out of 5 Stars! | Great Info

"I found the book very informative and a great guide to help me better understand my new puppy"

-D. Martillo

- ~ - ~ - ~ - - - ~ - ~ - - 5 Star Reviews - ~ - ~ - ~ - ~ -- ~ - ~ - ~ -

5.0 out of 5 Stars! | Great Info

"I have had three dogs, and this book was a great reference to go to when I needed help."

-Dotzee

- ~ - ~ - ~ - - - ~ - ~ - - 5 Star Reviews - ~ - ~ - ~ - ~ -- ~ - ~ - ~ -

5.0 out of 5 Stars! | Five Stars!

"Easy to read and understand, a fun read- and very informative"

-Woodland Steward

- ~ - ~ - ~ - - - ~ - ~ - - 5 Star Reviews - ~ - ~ - ~ - ~ -- ~ - ~ - ~ -

5.0 out of 5 Stars! | Very Good.

"Simple reading; anyone would benefit who has a new puppy in their life and wants a well behaved companion and friend"

-Arleen Lommers

- ~ - ~ - ~ - - - ~ - ~ - - 5 Star Reviews - ~ - ~ - ~ - ~ -- ~ - ~ - ~ -

- ~ - ~ - ~ - ~ - - - ~ - ~ - 5 Star Reviews - ~ - ~ - ~ - ~ -- ~ - ~ - ~ -

5.0 out of 5 Stars! | Five Stars!

"Great small book, that echoes the advice and training of professional dog instructors. Good value.

-GDH

- ~ - ~ - ~ - ~ - - - ~ - ~ - 5 Star Reviews - ~ - ~ - ~ - ~ -- ~ - ~ - ~ -

5.0 out of 5 Stars! | Great Info

"The information in this is wonderful and the author is funny he knows what he is talking about. And I was able to understand and apply it"

-Amazon Customer

- ~ - ~ - ~ - ~ - - - ~ - ~ - 5 Star Reviews - ~ - ~ - ~ - ~ -- ~ - ~ - ~ -

5.0 out of 5 Stars! | Very Helpful

"Enjoyed reading this book. I've picked up quite a few and this one definitely is high up on the list"

-Jennifer A. Bogucki

- ~ - ~ - ~ - ~ - - - ~ - ~ - 5 Star Reviews - ~ - ~ - ~ - ~ -- ~ - ~ - ~ -

5.0 out of 5 Stars! | Five Stars

"Great book"

-Joanne Fraties

- ~ - ~ - ~ - ~ - - - ~ - ~ - 5 Star Reviews - ~ - ~ - ~ - ~ -- ~ - ~ - ~ -

The Bearded Collie

Beardies are medium sized herding dogs from Scotland that were given the moniker "Bouncing Beardie" because when they are in thick underbrush they will bounce to get a clear view of the hillside and of the herds they are in charge. They are rough and tough dogs capable of withstanding all weather conditions. Their long double coat has a thick undercoat that keeps them cozy no matter rain, sleet, or snow. These dogs adore being outdoors and are healthiest when they have plenty of outdoor time along with rigorous exercise, but at night, they expect to be inside close to their families. Affectionate, fun loving, lively, and generally easy-going dogs that are known to always have a tail wagging, they get along well with children and as long as they are properly exercised they make terrific family pets.

As part of the Herding Group, they will tend to round up children, people, ducks, geese, and anything else that moves. Always supervise your dog when around children. This breed loves to be outdoors and working. This instinct cannot be trained away and their energy needs to be directed into sports, games, and play, so that their boundless energy has an outlet and their mental capacities are satisfied. They are an intelligent thinking breed and thus need proper stimulation. Beardies are a highly trainable breed that excels in a variety of dog sports, such as herding, agility, rally, and obedience.

The long Beardie coat will change as they make their way from puppy to adult. Sometime between nine and eighteen months the adult coat will begin growing in and replacing the puppy coat. During this transition, a little extra grooming will help keep matting from occurring. During coat maturation which lasts from two to four years to reach full length, your Beardies coat will change from darker to lighter color shades, possibly not showing its final coat color until age four. Usually the dog's eye color will match his coat color, with black and brown coats having brown eyes, grey coats having grey-blue eyes, and fawn colored Beardies have a light brown eye color that might have a touch of hazel or lavender.

You are a candidate to be a Beardie owner if you like energetic, intelligent dogs that respond well to training, and you know that you have plenty of time to spend in the company of your dog. Beardies crave human company and many negative behaviors can surface if they do not have their attention and exercise requirements met. With proper socialization, this breed usually gets along well with other pets and dogs.

History

As with all dog breeds that date back thousands of years, it is difficult to pinpoint the exact genesis of these old or ancient breeds of dogs. This holds true with the Bearded Collie as well. There are a few significant breeds that encompass similar characteristics of the Beardie, and thus a few theories prevail regarding their ancient heritage. How did this breed of dog land in Scotland ending up working as sheepherders in the Scottish Highlands? Many of the long coated sheepdogs may owe their heritage to the Hungarian Komondor of the Hungarian Magyars. The Komondor descended from the dogs of Tibet. It is believed that the original dogs were brought from Asia Minor when the Magyars headed west to conquer new lands. The Magyars of the Middle Ages were known for their incredible cavalry and bow forces. Sometime before the 9th century, they conquered, founded, and settled in what we call the Hungarian region and the country now named Hungary.

There is a common yarn that states that a trading ship that came from Poland in the early 1500's and had aboard herding dogs known as Lowland Polish Sheepdogs, which may owe their heritage to the Komondor. These dogs were then bred with the other Highland types of herding dogs that had arrived about three thousand years earlier. They were then put to use for herding and driving flocks to market. It is also known that the Romans brought dogs with them wherever they conquered lands and they may have brought along contributing dogs. The best guess scenario is that together with the ancient indigenous sheepdogs of the Scottish Highlands that date back five to seven thousand years, along with other transplanted dogs, we ended up with the Bearded Collie. Because there is almost no written history coming from Scotland until the eighteen hundreds, it makes it difficult to put forth a recent accurate historical record.

Known in the Highlands for centuries, they received very little outside attention until in 1912 a breed standard was drawn up. After that, they still remained fairly obscure until in 1959 a Beardie was shown, and became a champion. Afterward their popularity started to rise and the Bearded Collie Club of America was formed in 1969, and AKC recognized the breed in 1976.

Health

Like humans, dogs have the potential to develop ailments and diseases. Many of these ailments and diseases vary from breed to breed, and some are more prevalent, occurring more often in certain breeds. Consider these facts when picking out your new puppy, and beware of any breeder that makes a claim that their type of breed puppies are 100% healthy. A reputable and honest breeder should know and share any health related issues that the breed you are purchasing or inquiring about might have, or can potentially surface.

Bearded Collies are a healthy breed but have a few potential ailments. The possible health issues of the Bearded Collie, include hip and elbow dysplasia, eye diseases, Addison's disease, pemphigus foliaceous skin disease, and autoimmune thyroiditis.

I recommend reading about canine health related issues and common breed specific ailments. By becoming familiar with the signs and symptoms of a disease or sickness, you will be empowered to be the first line of defense in support of your dog's health and wellbeing. Routine physical examinations of your dog, inspection of feces, and noting food related issues that cause bowel or gastric problems helps to assure him or her enjoying optimal health. By observing and understanding your dog's healthy behaviors and regular patterns, you will be able to easily identify when your dog is not feeling well, and if medical attention is needed.

In your position and role as alpha, you are responsible for providing the best possible care for your dog, assuring his or her wellbeing and comfort. Do not hesitate to consult your veterinarian if you observe your dog displaying peculiar behaviors or showing any signs of discomfort. It is very important to maintain your dog's scheduled exams, mandatory check up's and vaccination appointments. Uphold this duty, so that your dog can enjoy the vitality of good health that he or she deserves, and in fact has a right too.

Long daily walks are recommended for having a healthy dog. Walks promote leash training practice, socialization, and over-all mental and physical health for your dog to satisfy its pack mentality needs.

Feeding Your Bearded Collie

Age, weight, and activity levels are a few of the factors that can change the food requirements of your Beardie. Once you have determined the appropriate amount to provide, feed an accurately measured portion at regular times to help maintain their optimal weight. If you wish to feed your dog a raw food diet or a mix, please do your research and consult your veterinarian prior to any adjustments to their meals. Be sure to keep plenty of fresh, clean water available for your dog, and it is considered a hygienic standard to clean your dog's bowl well, after each feeding.

Proactive Measures for Puppy Selection

If you want to buy a Bearded Collie puppy, be sure to find a reputable Beardie puppy breeder who will show you health clearances for both of the puppy's parents. Health clearances are official documents that prove a dog has been tested for, and cleared of any, or all breed specific conditions, however a clearance does not guarantee against acquired diseases or abnormalities. Remember, even under the best breeding practices and proactive care measures, puppies can still develop diseases.

For the Bearded Collie breed, you should expect to see a health clearance from the Orthopedic Foundation for Animals (OFA) for hip dysplasia, and autoimmune thyroiditis, as well as a clearance from the Canine Eye Registry Foundation (CERF), certifying that the eyes are healthy. You can also confirm health clearances by checking the OFA web site (offa.org).

The American Kennel Club (AKC) conducts large canine research studies on diseases that affect purebred dogs. Their health program is the Canine Health Foundation (CHF). This foundation, in partnership with OFA, has a breed testing designation called the Canine Health Information Center (CHIC). The results of these tests are maintained in a registry, and dogs that have all the required exams, including tests of the hips, elbows, and eyes, receive a CHIC number. Along with the breed-testing program, there is the CHIC DNA Repository. CHIC is trying to gather and store breed DNA samples for canine disease research. The goal is to facilitate future research aimed at reducing the incidence of inherited diseases in dogs. You can search the database to find out if a specific dog has information listed about it. More information about CHIC is available here: http://www.caninehealthinfo.org

To be accepted into the CHIC database, breeders must agree to have all test results published. This enables the reader to see both good and bad results of the testing. Obtaining a CHIC number does not imply that the dog received good or passing evaluation scores. The CHIC registration also does not signify as proof of the absence of disease, and all information must be read and evaluated. CHIC allows the information collected to be readily available to anyone with an inquiry.

The Orthopedic Foundation for Animals (OFA www.offa.org) maintains an open registry with evaluations of hips, elbows, eyes, thyroid, cardio and other canine health issues. PennHIP (www.pennhip.org) is another registry that also evaluates dog's hips.

Care

You are responsible for the welfare of your new puppy or dog. Please treat him or her with respect and love, and this will be reciprocated tenfold. Dogs have been human companions for thousands of years, and they are living beings complete with feelings, emotions and the need for attachment. Before bringing home a new dog or puppy, please determine if you are capable and willing to provide all that your new family member will need.

From the time you bring your pup home, positive training is a great start to introducing your new pack member to your household. Dogs have an amazing capacity to remember experiences, so please refrain from harsh training tactics that may intimidate your puppy and negatively affect personality or demeanor. When you train your new puppy, give him or her the respect they deserve and utilize all available positive reinforcements, and as a result your dog will amaze you with surprising abilities, traits, and characteristics that are buried within the genetic profile of their specific breed. I am an advocate for beginning with rewards based clicker training, followed by vocal and physical cues for your young dog to learn, and then obey.

Crate training has positive benefits, and provides a safe place for your dog to nap or simply to be alone. In addition, crate training at a young age will help your dog accept confinement if he ever needs to be transported, boarded or hospitalized.

Proper, early, and ongoing socialization will help you and your Beardie throughout his or her lifetime. Expose your new puppy or dog to a wide variety of situations, people, and animals. This prevents shyness, aggressiveness, possessiveness, and many other potential behavioral problems, meanwhile supporting the bond between the two of you. Never leave young children unsupervised around dogs or puppies, and remember that situations of aggression may happen no matter how loving, gentle, and well trained a dog may be.

Follow a scheduled basic care program for your dog so that his coat, nails, teeth, and general health aspects are always done in a timely and efficient manner. They have a long double coat that requires daily brushing to keep tangles and mats away, but you can get away with three or four times a week. Eyes, ears, and paws should be regularly inspected and tended too. The long outer coat requires diligent attention and their thick undercoat requires inspection for ticks and any other critter finding a home. Misting the coat before brushing keeps from damaging the hair, do not be afraid to have a professional show you the proper technique for taking care of an adult Beardie coat. It is your personal decision as to the cut you wish your Beardie to wear. Many prefer to trim the facial hair to display their friendly furry face or use a top knot.

Training

Herding dogs are bred to be intelligent and independent dogs. Beardies include those two traits and are also sensitive and intuitive to human's moods and actions. Because of this, you need to pay attention to how you are feeling before and during training sessions so that your dog does not notice any negative energy such as frustration, tiredness, or anger. Beardies are sometimes labeled stubborn, but that is their independence and intellect mulling over whether the action being asked of them is worth doing, rather than not learning or refusing to learn. When focused they learn and retain quickly. Beardies enjoy play, fun, and variety in all things, so this should be immersed into your training sessions. Offer a wide variety of treats, lots of praise, play with their favorite toys, maybe some fetch after a training session.

Understanding your Beardie will greatly help you in training. Be patient, positive, firm, but fair during your training and living with your puppy. As mentioned many times throughout this guide, begin socialization early and continue throughout their lifetime. Reward the positive actions and ignore the negative actions. Pay close attention to unwanted nipping, and show your puppy early that it is painful and not tolerated by humans. Beardies are jumpers and that is another behavior to pay attention so that this hefty dog does not jump up onto family, friends, and guests. Begin handling training when you bring your little furry puppy home. You will be spending a lot of time grooming and handling your Beardie, having a dog that is used to and enjoys being handled makes grooming and other care much easier and safer.

Bearded Collies compete in tracking, obedience, herding, agility, and conformation shows; additionally they are used as therapy dogs.

To begin training, establish your *alpha position* from the moment you bring home your new dog or puppy, then begin training the basics around six weeks to eight weeks age. Once your puppy realizes that you control schedules, toys, mealtimes and all the things he or she cherishes, he or she will respect you as the alpha in the family hierarchy. Remember that all family members are above your dog. Leading as the alpha assists in working together with your dog towards the goal of understanding the rules of conduct and obedience. Your dog will be at ease when the rules are understood. Put your puppy on a schedule for feeding, potty times, walks and more. Be in control of toys and play time so that your Beardie understands that you control all good things. This is important, because if your puppy doesn't have this structure early he or she will grow up thinking that they can do as they wish. No matter how wonderful and easy- going your little Beardie seems now, most likely that will change with age.

Begin gradually socializing your puppy from the time you bring him or her home. Proper early socialization that continues throughout your puppy's lifetime will provide you with a well-adjusted dog that is able to handle almost any situation in a calm manner. Early, thorough, and continual socialization is important for your Beardie. You do not want your dog being territorial and wary of strangers, so it is important to expose them early to a variety of situations, animals, people, and places. Socialization benefits you and your dog by providing you with a peace of mind and that you can expose your Beardie to different situations with the assurance that he or she will look to you for guidance in rules of etiquette for the indoor and outdoor world. Socialization is a foundation for all dogs throughout their lifetimes.

Training should always be an enjoyable bonding time between you and your dog. Remember that all dogs are different, and that there is no set time limit for when your dog should learn, understand, and properly obey commands. Always have fun during training, remembering to keep your training sessions short and stop if either of you are tired or distracted. I always suggest beginning training new tricks or commands in an area of least distraction. I promote starting with rewards based clicker training and ending with vocal and or physical cues for your dog to follow.

If you notice any negative behavioral issues and are not quite sure if you are offering your dog the proper socialization and training necessary, do not hesitate to enter your puppy into a puppy kindergarten class to assist you with your training and socialization. The time to enroll your puppy is usually around eight to ten weeks of age and after their first round of shots, although some kindergarten classes will not accept puppies until they are three to four months of age.

Reward good behaviors, but do not reward for being cute, sweet, loveable, or huggable. If you wish to reward your dog, always reward after you issue a command and your dog obeys the command. During your training sessions, be sure to mix it up, add a variety of toys and treats, and do not forget to have fun. Remember to provide them with ample daily exercise to keep them fit, healthy, and to keep behavioral problems at bay. Provide consistent structure, firm authority, rule enforcement, love and affection, and you will have one heck of a dog for you and your family.

Enjoy your Bearded Collie!

More: **Bearded Collie Facts**

Introduction

Who is "man's best friend?" My wife says it's the couch, a pizza and ESPN, but that is because she grew up with four brothers. However, we all know man's best friend is his dog. I love my dog. I love dogs. They provide comfort, support, undying love, and someone to bounce all those brilliant ideas off that are going to make you a millionaire someday. I cannot imagine life without my dog.

When I picked Axel up and brought him home, he was a puppy. I was advised to train him well and not to make him a guard or an attack dog. Actually, training your dog makes him happier, healthier, and much more stable. Who knew?

With that in mind, I embarked on the journey of training this little puppy. Diving in head first, I bought books, acquired videos, and even talked with professional trainers about the matter. Over time, I gleaned a lot of helpful information. I learned about commonly encountered behavioral problems, and some not so common as well. I absorbed facts about proper diet, exercise, and training techniques. Because of my interest and commitment to his best interest, my dog is well behaved, happy, social, and understands a point spread better than any other dog traveling in the car pool lane.

While I was going through the process of learning how to train my puppy, I noticed one thing; *trainers are really, really,* serious about their craft, but will my lack of seriousness result in a poorly trained dog? The informality of my approach has resulted in a fabulous companion that clumsily bumps around the house, and chews on this and that in pure puppy form. Whether he's curled up snoozing or striking an adorable pose, the real joy comes simply from his mere presence, and of these joys, the laughter that he incites is at the very top of the list.

Keeping laughter and light heartedness in mind as a dog owner in training, is of the utmost importance because sometimes training can be very difficult on you and your pal. Sometimes your dog will push your patience to the limits. Remember to try and never let your dog know that you are at your limits. You are given the awesome responsibility at the time of acquisition, to be the pack leader and ultimately your dog's sensei.

I kept that in mind when I sat down to put this rewards based training book together. What I hope you will find inside here is a complete, concise training guide, the information of which is culled from trainers, training manuals and years of experience with a wonderful dog. Though this guide approaches training as a serious endeavor, your dog will teach you that it will not always be serious, and nor should you. I have attempted to infuse his playful spirit throughout this instructional. I hope that those light moments within this reading will help you get through the tougher times, like the chewing of your cell phone, the pooping on your socks and those mysterious expenses charged to your credit card. "Could it be that only Axel is able to run a credit card via telephone?"

A dog can be a loyal and longtime friend, worthy of your commitment and care. Your dog can give your life so much richness, and in return, asks very little. If you train your dog well, he or she will be happier, and as science has proven, so will you. If you keep a sense of humor alive during training, the outcomes will be the best for both of you. I hope you find this guide informative, easy to follow and fun. Enjoy.

Table of Contents

Getting Social with Your Beardie

Socializing your puppy, especially before the age of six months, is a very important step in preventing future behavioral problems. Socializing can and should continue throughout the life of your dog. Socializing in a gentle and kind manner prevents aggressive, fearful, and potential behaviors with possible litigious outcomes. A lack of socializing may lead to *fear, aggression, barking*, shyness, *destruction*, territorialism, or *hyperactivity*, and the risk of *wearing Goth make up and the smoking of clove cigarettes*. The earlier you start socializing, the better. However, all puppies and dogs can gradually be brought into new and initially frightening situations, eventually learning to enjoy them. Canines can adapt to various and sometimes extreme situations, they just need your calm, guiding hand.

Expect that the socializing of your dog will be a lifelong endeavor. If your puppy does not engage with other dogs for months or years at a time, you can expect his behavior to be different when he encounters them again. I mean, how would you feel if your sixth grade math teacher, who you haven't seen in 22 years, just walked up and sniffed you?

Here are some methods you can use when exposing your dog to something new, or something he has previously been distrustful contacting:

- Remain calm, upbeat and if he has a leash on, keep it loose.

- Gradually expose him to the new stimulus and if he is wary or fearful never use force. Let him retreat if he needs to.

- Reward you dog using treats; give him a good scratch or an energetic run for being calm and exploring new situations.

Try on a regular basis to expose your dog to the things that you would like him to be capable to cope. His gained familiarity will allow him to calmly deal with such situations in the future. Be careful of the same old-same old. Though dogs love routine, periodically expose your dog to new things. This allows you to assess his need for further socialization. You certainly wouldn't want to go on vacation to the same place every single year, so why would he.

Examples of situations that benefit the social temperament of your Beardie:

- Meeting new kinds of people, including but not limited to, children, crowds, people wearing hats, disabled folks, and people in local services such as postal carriers, fire and police officers, and more. "Introducing your puppy to a circus clown is saved for another chapter."

- Meeting new dogs is encouraged. Because of canine diseases, be aware that you should wait at least 4 months before introducing your puppy to dog parks or places where there are groups of adult dogs. You can begin puppy socialization classes at around 7 weeks, just be sure your puppy has a round of vaccines at least a week prior. Slowly expose your dog to other pets, such as cats, horses, birds, llamas, pigs, gerbils, and monitor lizards.

- Your dog's crate is not a jail. Be sure and take the time to teach your puppy to enjoy the comfort and privacy of his own crate. You want your dogs crate to be a place that he or she feels safe. We will be going over instructions on this in the section, Housetraining.

What, Where, When, Why

Everyone reads or hears socialization mentioned when reading about dogs and puppies. What is the reason for socialization? When is the best time to socialize my shiny new puppy? These and more, are questions you often hear asked. Does it has to do with getting along well with other dogs and people or is there more to it? Do I let them loose with other dogs and puppies, and just sit back, and watch? Let us begin by looking at how a puppy's social development process is played out from puppy to adulthood.

Socialization is learning and maintaining acceptable behavior in any situation, especially when your dog or puppy does not want too. The goal is learning to handle any normal experience that occurs in life without becoming overly stimulated, fearful, reactive, or aggressive. You want your dog to be able to go with the flow, keep centered, and calm, no matter what the circumstance.

Socialization summary

- *Learning to remain calm when the world is buzzing around them.*

- *Exposure in a safe manner to the environment that will encompass his or her world, including the rules and guidelines that accompany it.*

3

- Learning to respond to signals when they do not want too. For example, In the midst of a tail chasing session with a fellow puppy or the irresistible squirrel.

The first phase of socialization begins as early as 3 weeks and lasts to approximately 12 weeks old, during this time puppies discover that they are dogs and begin to play with their littermates. Survival techniques that they will use throughout their lives, such as biting, barking, chasing, and fighting, begin to be acted out. Concurrently during this time-period, puppies experience big changes socially and physically. Learning submissive postures and taking corrections from their mother, interaction with their littermates begin to teach them about hierarchies. Keeping mother and puppies together for at least 7 weeks tends to increase their ability to get along well with other dogs and learn more about themselves and their actions, such as the force of a bite on their brothers and sisters.

Between the ages of 7-12 weeks, a period of rapid learning occurs and they learn what humans are, and whether to accept them as safe. This is a crucial period, and has the *greatest impact* on *all future social behavior*. This is the time we begin teaching puppies the acceptable rules of conduct. Take note that they have a short attention span, and physical limitations. This is the easiest period to get your puppy comfortable with new things, and the chance to thwart later behavioral issues that stem from improper or incomplete socialization. Puppies are not out of harm's way from all diseases at this time, but the risk is relatively low because of primary vaccines, good care, and mother's milk immunity. Behavioral problems are the greatest threat to the owner-dog bond and the number one cause of death to dogs under 3 years of age.

Enrolling your puppy in classes before 3 months of age is an outstanding avenue to improving socialization, training, and strengthening the bond between you and your puppy. You can begin socialization classes as early as 7-8 weeks. The recommendation is to have your puppy receive at least 1 set of vaccines, and a de-worming 7 days prior to starting the first class.

From birth, puppies should be exposed to handling and manipulation of body parts, and exposure to different people, places, situations, well socialized animals, and more. Encourage your puppies exploring, curiosity, and investigation of different environments. Games, toys, and a variety of surfaces such as steps, tile, concrete, tunnels, are all things to expose your puppy too and should continue into adulthood to keep your dog sociable and not shy.

It is important for your puppy to be comfortable playing, sleeping, or exploring alone. Schedule alone play with toys, and solo naps in their crate or another safe area. This teaches them to entertain themselves and not become overly attached, or have separation issues with their owners. Getting them comfortable with their crate is also beneficial for travel and to use as a safe area for your puppy to relax and feel safe.

Having knowledge of your breed and puppy will help in understanding their social predispositions. Some breeds that act as sporting and companion dogs will carry puppy sociability into adulthood. Terriers, guard, herding, and *bully* dogs become less tolerant while others consistently challenge or remain passive. Which is your breed's disposition?

Two phases of fear imprinting occur in your growing puppy's life. *A fear period is a stage during which your puppy or dog may be more apt to perceive certain stimuli as threatening.* During these two periods, any event your puppy thinks is traumatic can leave a lasting effect, possibly forever. The first period is from 8-11 weeks and the second is between 6-14months of age. During this period, you will want to keep your puppy clear of any frightening situations, but that is not always easy to determine. A chrome balloon on the floor could possibly scare the "bejeebers" out of your little pup. There is no one size fits all here in knowing what is fearful for your puppy. Becoming familiar with canine body language can help you diagnose your pups fear factor. The second period often reflects the dog becoming more reactive or apprehensive about new things. Larger breeds sometimes have an extended second period.

Keep a few things in mind when seeking play dates for socialization of your puppy. A stellar puppy class will have a safe, mature dog for the puppies to learn boundaries and other behaviors. When making play dates, puppies should be matched by personality and play styles. Games, such as retrieve or drop, help to curb possessive behaviors, as well as to help them learn to give up unsafe or off limits items, so that the item can be taken out of harm's way. Another important lesson during play is for puppies to learn to come back to their human. *Your dog should be willingly dependent upon you and look to you for guidance.*

Teach mature easily stimulated dogs to relax before they are permitted to socialize with others. If you have an adult dog that enjoys flying solo, do not force them into situations. Teach your dogs and puppies less aroused play and encourage passive play. This includes play that does not encompass dominance, mouthing, or biting other puppies. If you have rough play happening between multiple dogs or puppies, then interrupt the rough housing by frequently calling them to you and rewarding their attention. The attention then is turned to you. As a distraction to dissuade mouthing contact, try to interject toys into the play. Elevated play can lead to aggression as they grow, especially breeds that can easily get to full arousal in seconds.

Proper socialization requires patience, kindness, and consistency while teaching. You and your dog should both be having fun during this process. Allow your dog to proceed into new situations at his or her own pace, never force them into a situation that they are not comfortable. If you think that your dog may have a socialization issue, seek professional advice from a qualified behavioral person.

"Well! That's Not Good Behavior!"

How to deal with a problem behavior before it becomes a habit

Everyone likes his or her own space to feel comfy, familiar, and safe. Your dog is no different. A proper living space is a key factor to avoiding all kinds of potential problems. Think of all the things your puppy will encounter in his life with humans. Things like baths, walks, radio, T.V., neighbors, visitors, household appliance noises, construction, engines, lawnmowers, and so forth that are not necessarily familiar or common in nature, and can be frightening to your dog. It is essential to use treats, toys, and praise to assist you and your dog while in the midst of training and socializing.

Dogs are social creatures and it is essential to communicate with them. Communication is always the key to behavior reinforcement. Showing your dog that calm behavior is frequently rewarded, and that you have control over his favorite things, acts as a pathway to solving problems that may arise down the road.

Keep your dog's world happy. Make sure he is getting a proper amount of exercise and that he is being challenged mentally. Make sure he is getting enough time in the company of other dogs and other people. Keep a close eye on his diet, offering him good, healthy, dog-appropriate foods. A small treat every now and then is perfectly in order. Avoid excessive helpings when treating.

It is important that you be a strong leader. Dogs are pack animals and your dog needs to know that you are the alpha. Do not let situations fall into that questionable "who's the boss?" scenario. Your puppy will feel confident and strong if he works for his rewards and knows that he or she has a strong, confident leader to follow. Let your dog show you good behavior before you pile on the goodies, or a new roof on his doghouse. With a little work on his part, he will appreciate it more.

Getting by the challenges

Your dog's first step towards overcoming the challenges in life is in understanding what motivates his own behavior. Some behaviors your dog will exhibit are instinctual. Chewing, barking, digging, jumping, chasing, digging, and leash pulling are things that all dogs do because it is in their genetic make-up. These natural behaviors differ from the ones we have inadvertently trained into the domestic canine. Behaviors such as nudging our hands asking to be petted, or barking for attention, are actually accidently reinforced by us humans and not innate.

What motivates your dog to do what he does or does not do? You may wonder why he does not come when you call him while he is playing with other dogs. Simply, this may be because coming to you is far less exciting than scrapping with the same species. When calling your dog you can change this behavior simply by offering him a highly coveted treat and after treating, allow him to continue playing for a while. Start this training aspect slowly, and in short distances from where he is playing. Gradually increase the distances and distractions when you beckon your dog.

Here are some helpful tips to use when trying to help your Bearded Collie through challenging behavior.

- Are you accidentally rewarding bad behavior? Remember that your dog may see any response from you as a reward. You can ignore the misbehavior if you are patient enough, or you can give your puppy the equivalent of a human *time out* for a few minutes. Make sure the time out environment is in a calm, quiet and safe, but very dull place, similar to my grandma's condo in Florida. More on time outs later inside this guide.

- Think about the quality of his diet and health. Is your dog getting enough playtime, mental and physical exercise, and sleep? Is this a medical problem? Do not ignore the range of possibilities that could be eliciting your dog's challenging behavior.

- Be sure and practice replacement behavior. Reward him with something that is much more appealing than the perceived reward that he is getting when he is misacting. It is important to reward his good behavior before he misacts. If done consistently and correctly, this will reinforce good behaviors, and reduce poor behaviors.

For example, in the hopes of receiving love, your dog is repeatedly nudging your hand; teach him to *sit* instead by only giving him love after he sits, and never if he nudges you. If you command, "sit" and he complies, and then you pat him on the head or speak nicely to him, or both, your dog will associate the sitting compliance with nice things. If he nudges and you turn away and never acknowledge him he will understand that behavior is not associated with nice things. In a scenario where your dog is continually nudging you for attention, you want to catch him before he comes running into your room and begins nudging, and then, immediately say, "sit."

- While practicing the replacement behavior, be sure you reward the right response and ignore the mistakes. Remember, any response to the wrong action could be mistaken as a reward by your dog, so try to remain neutral in a state of ignoring, this includes, sight, touch and verbal acknowledgement. Be sure to offer your dog a greater reward for the correct action than the joy he is getting from doing the wrong action. You will have to think up counter actions for each wrong action you are replacing.

- Your dog's bad behavior may be caused by something that causes him fear. If you decipher this as the problem try to change his mind about what he perceives frightening. Pair the scary thing with something he loves. Say your dog has a problem with the local skateboarder. Pair the skateboarder's visit with a super treat and lots of attention. He will soon look forward to the daily arrival of the skateboarder.

- Always, remain patient with your dog and do not force changes. Work gradually and slowly. Forcing behavioral changes on your dog may lead to making the behaviors worse. Training requires that you work as hard as your dog, and maybe harder, because you have to hone your observational skills, intuition, timing, patience, laughter, and the understanding of your dog's body language and demeanor.

~ Paws On – Paws Off ~

Things That Work While Training

Knowing what you want to train your dog to do is as important as training your dog. You can begin training almost immediately, at around six weeks of age. A puppy is a blank slate and does not know any rules, therefore it is a wise idea to make a list and have an understanding of what you would like your puppy to do. What are the household rules and proper dog etiquette? As he grows, the same principle applies and you may adjust training from the basics to more specialized behaviors, such as making your dog a good travel, hiking, agility, hunting, or simply a companion dog. Know what conditions and circumstances you plan to expose your dog or puppy to outside of the household and strategize to be prepared for those encounters by slowly introducing your dog to those situations.

Establish yourself as the pack leader from the time you first bring your new dog or puppy home. Being the *alpha* assists in the training process, and your dogs relationship with you and your family. Life is much easier for your dog if you are in charge, leading, and providing for his needs. Leading as the alpha assists in the act of working together with your dog towards the goal of understanding the rules of conduct and obedience. Your dog will be at ease when the rules are understood. Training should be an enjoyable bonding time between you and your dog. Remember that there is no set time limit defining when your dog should learn, understand, and then obey commands. Use short training sessions and be aware that if either of you are tired, it is recommended that you stop and try again later. If something does not seem quite right with your dog, in any way, have him checked out by a veterinarian.

Timing is crucial when rewarding for good behaviors and making corrections for bad. *Patience and Consistency* are your allies in the training game. An easy way to avoid the onset of many different behavioral problems is to give your dogs or puppies ample daily exercise to keep them fit and healthy, and destructive behavioral problems at bay. Always provide consistent structure, firm but fair authority, rule enforcement, and importantly, love and affection. By maintaining these things, you will help to create a loyal companion and friend. Reward good behaviors, not for simply being cute, sweet, loveable, and huggable. If you wish to reward your dog, always reward after you issue a command and your dog obeys appropriately.

Only train one command per session. Puppies and some breeds only have the attention span to go about 10 minutes per session, but never exceed 15 minutes. Training a command once per day is enough for your dog to begin to learn and retain, but whenever the opportunity presents itself you should reinforce the training sessions throughout the day. For example, opening a door or putting down a food bowl first command sit, down or stay and be sure not to reward your dog unless your dog obeys. The most important thing to remember is to remain relaxed, keep it fun, and enjoy this time of bonding and training your dog or puppy.

All dogs have their own personalities and therefore respond to training differently. No matter the breed that usually comes with its own characteristics, you need to account for individual personality and adjust accordingly. If needed, do not hesitate to solicit professional help and advice.

We all love treats, and so does your dog. Giving your dog a treat is the best way to reinforce good behavior, to help change his behavior or just to make your dog do that insanely funny dance- like-thing he does. Make the treats small enough for him to get a taste, but not a meal, kernel sized. Remember, you do not want him filling up on treats as it might spoil his dinner and interfere with his attention span.

- Keep a container of treats handy with you at all times. You do not want to miss a chance to reward a good behavior or reinforce a changed behavior. Always carry treats when you go on a walk. Remember what treats your dog likes most and save those for super special times. In addition, what you consider a treat and what your dog considers a treat are two vastly different worlds. A single malt scotch or chicken wings might be a treat in your mind, but dried liver bits or beef jerky in your dogs.

- Ask for something before you give the treat. Tell your dog to sit, stay, or lie down, print two copies of your resume, anything, before you reward your dog with treats, petting, or play. By asking for good behavior, before you give your dog a reward, you demonstrate you are in charge, in an easy fun manner. There is a common misconception that dogs are selfless and wanting to behave only to please out of respect for you. This is horse pucky. This line of thinking is incorrect and detrimental to your success with the training. You have to make sure that your dog knows exactly why he should be listening to you. You are the alpha, the keeper of the treats, the provider of the scratching and the purveyor of toys. Keep this balance of power and the results will be your reward.

- Be positive. Think about what you want your dog to do, instead of what you don't want him to do. Do not send mixed messages. Simply, ignore the bad behavior and reward your dog when he does the action you request to be done. Teach your dog some simple commands to communicate what you want, such as, "drop it," or "leave it."

- Keep the training sessions short at 15 minutes maximum per session. You will be continuously training your companion, but use the formal training sessions to focus on one objective. Any session longer than 15 minutes will be hard for your dog to stay focused. During training, this is the attention span of most canines. Ten minutes per session is a good time limit for young puppies. Some breeds stay puppies longer than others stay, and may not fully develop until year two. Use a variety and an abundance of different treats and rewards. Rewards are play, toys, praise, affection, treats, and anything that you know that your dog enjoys.

- Run, run, run! It is understood that your dog will be much happier if you run your dog every day. Run your dog until his tongue is hanging out. If he is still full of energy, run him again and he will love you for this. Before a training session begins, use a little exercise to release some of your dog's energy, this can increase his ability to focus during the session. Toy and many small dogs do not require excessive exercise but still require daily walks and play sessions.

- It is very important that you make sure your dog is comfortable in all sorts of situations. All dogs, even your sweet tempered Beardie, have the potential to bite. Making sure, he is comfortable in various situations and teaching your dog to be gentle with his mouth will reduce the risk of unwanted bites. Mouthing should not be acceptable behavior because it leads to worse actions.

- Kids are great, are they not? However, the notion that kids and dogs are as natural a pairing as chocolate and peanut butter is simply not true. Kids are often bitten by dogs because they unintentionally do things that frighten dogs. Sometimes a child's behavior appears like prey to a dog. Never leave a dog and a child together unsupervised, even if the dog is *good* with children. Teach children not to approach a dog that is unfamiliar to them. The way a child behaves with the familiar family dog, may not be appropriate with another dog that they meet for the first time. Instruct children that tail pulling, hugging their necks tightly, leg pulling, and hard head pats are not acceptable.

~ Paws On – Paws Off ~

Rewards not Punishment

It is always better to reward your Beardie instead of punishing him or her. Here are a few reasons why:

- If you punish your dog, it can make him distrust, or cause fear, aggression, and avoidance of you. If you rub your dog's nose his doodie or pee, he may avoid going to the bathroom in front of you. This is going to make his public life difficult.

- Physical punishment has the tendency to escalate in severity. If you get your dog's attention by a light tap on the nose, he will soon get used to that and ignore it. Shortly the contact will become more and more violent. As we know, violence is *not* the answer.

- Punishing your dog may have some bad side effects. For example, if you are using a pinch collar, it may tighten when he encounters other dogs. Dogs are very smart, but they are not always logical. When your dog encounters another dog, the pinching of the collar may lead him to think that the other dog is the reason for the pinch. *Pinch collars have been linked to the reinforcement of aggressive behaviors between dogs.*

- Electric fences will make him avoid the yard.

- Choke collars can cause injuries to a dog's throat as well as cause back and neck misalignment.

- You may inadvertently develop and adversarial relationship with your dog if you punish your dog instead of working through a reward system and correctly leading. If you only look for the mistakes within your dog, this is all you will begin to see. In your mind, you will see a problem dog. In your dog's mind, he will see anger and distrust.

- You ultimately want to shape your dog's incorrect actions into acceptable actions. By punishing your dog, he will learn only to *avoid* punishment. He is not learning to change the behavior you want changed, instead he learns to be sneaky or to do the very minimum to avoid being punished. Your dog can become withdrawn and seemingly inactive. Permanent psychological damage can be done if a dog lives in fear of punishment.

- If you punish rather than reward neither you nor your dog will be having a very good time. It will be a constant, sometimes painful struggle. If you have children, they will not be able to participate in a punishment based training process because it is too difficult, and truly no fun.

- Simply put, if you train your dog using rewards, you and your dog will have a much better time and relationship. Rely on rewards to change his behavior by using treats, toys, playing, petting, affection, or anything else you know your dog likes. If your dog is doing something that you do not like, replace the habit with another by teaching your dog to do something different, and then reward him or her for doing the replacement action, and then you can all enjoy the outcome.

~ Paws On – Paws Off ~

Clicker Training Your Beardie

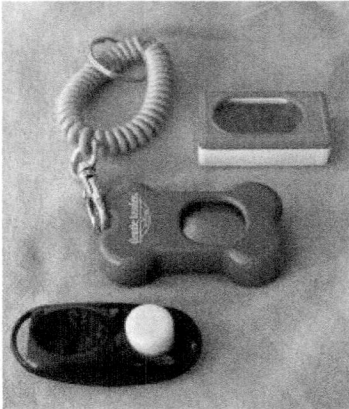

What the heck is that clicking noise? Well, it's a clicker, thus the name. If you are a product of a Catholic school, you might be very familiar with this device. You probably have nightmares of large, penguin like women clicking their way through your young life. Yes, it was annoying and at times, terrifying, however, when it comes to training your dog, it will be helpful and fun.

A clicker is a small device that makes a sound that is easily distinguished and not common as a sound in nature, or one that humans normally produce. This unique sound keeps the dog that is being trained from becoming confused by accidently hearing a word used in conversation or another environmental noise. You click at the exact time when your dog does the correct action then immediately follow the click with a treat or reward.

The clicker is used to inform your dog that he did the right thing and that a treat is coming. When your dog does the right thing after you command, like drop your Chanel purse that is dangling from his mouth, you click and reward him with a nice treat. Using the clicker system allows you to set your puppy up to succeed while you ignore or make efforts to prevent bad behavior. It is a very positive, humane system, and punishment is *not* part of the process.

Here are some questions often asked about the clicker training:

- "Do you need to have the clicker on your person at all times?" *No.* The clicker is a teaching device. Once your dog understands what you want your dog to do, you can then utilize a verbal or hand cue, and if inclined verbal praise or affection.

- "Can rewards be other things besides treats?" *Sure.* Actually, you should mix it up. Use the clicker and a treat when you first start teaching. When your puppy has learned the behavior you want, then switch to other rewards, such as, petting, play, toys, or lottery tickets. Remember always to ask for the wanted target behavior, such as, *sit*, *stay*, or *come,* before you reward your dog. These verbal reinforcements can augment the clicker training and reward giving.

- "With all these treats, isn't my dog going to get fat?" *No.* If you figure treats into your dog's daily intake and subtract from meals accordingly, your dog will be fine. The treats should be as small as a corn kernel, just a taste. Use food from his regular meals when you are training indoors, but when outdoors, use fresh treats like meat or cheese. There are many distractions outside and a tasty fresh treat will help keep your puppy's attention. Dog's finally honed senses will smell even the smallest of treat, and this keeps them attentive. -"What do I do if my dog doesn't act out the command?" *Simple*, if your dog disobeys you, it is because he has not been properly trained yet. Do not C/T (Click and Treat), or verbally praise for any wrong actions, ignore the wrong action. Continue training because your dog has not yet learned the command and action you are teaching him to perform. He, after all, is just a dog. If he is disobeying, he has been improperly or incompletely trained, maybe the treats are not tasty enough. Try simplifying the task and attempt to make the reward equal to, or better than what is distracting your dog. Eventually your dog will understand what action should be performed when the command word is spoken.

HELPFUL HINT

- *Conceal the treat! Do NOT* show your dog the treat before pressing the clicker and making the clicking sound. If you do this, he will be responding to the treat and not the click and this will *undermine* your training strategy.

Why and How Clicker Training Works

The important reason I put this information together is that it is essential to understand why timing and consistency is important, and why clicker training works. If any of this is confusing, do not worry, because I walk you through the training process, step-by-step.

Clicker training started over seventy years ago and has become a tried and true method for training dogs and other animals. The outcome of using a clicker is an example of conditioned reinforcement. Rewarding the animal in combination with clicker use has proven highly effective as a positive reinforcement training method. It is a humane and effective way of training dogs without instilling fear for non-compliance. I know that my mother wished she would have known about clicker training when my brother and I were growing up. I am sure she would have put the clicker into action so my brother would place his dirty clothes inside the bin, rather than on the floor.

In the 1950s, Keller Breland, a pioneer in animal training, used a clicker while training many different species of animals, including marine mammals. He met great success using this method of training on these animals. His system developed for clicker training marine mammals is still in use today. Keller also trained dogs using the clicker. Because of its effectiveness, it was brought into use by others in the dog training community. Gradually, clicker training for dogs gained more and more popularity and by the early 1980's its use became widespread. The success of the clicker spans 7 decades and now is a widely accepted standard for dog training.

A trainer will use the clicker to mark desired actions as they occur. At the exact instant, the animal performs the desired action, the trainer clicks and promptly delivers a food reward or other reinforcements. One key to clicker training is the trainer's timing, as *timing is crucial*. For example, clicking and rewarding slightly too early or too late will reinforce the action that is occurring at that very instant rather than the action you were targeting the reward for. The saying goes, "you get what you click for."

Clicker trainers often use the process of *shaping*. Shaping is the process of gradual transformation of a specific action into the desired action by rewarding each successive progression towards the desired action. This is done by gradually molding or training the dog to perform a specific response by first, reinforcing the small, successive responses that are similar to the desired response, instead of waiting for the perfect completion to occur. The trainer looks for small progressions that are heading in the direction towards the total completion of the desired action and then clicks and treats. It is important to recognize and reward those tiny steps made in the target direction. During training, the objective is to create opportunities for your dog to earn frequent rewards. In the beginning, it is acceptable to increase the frequency of a C/T to every 3-4 seconds, or less. By gauging the dog's abilities and improvements, the trainer can gradually increase the length of time between C/T. It is necessary to assess the dog's progress from moment to moment, adjusting C/T to achieve the desired actionable outcome.

During training, and in conjunction with clicker use, the introduction of a cue word or hand signal can be applied. Eventually, the clicker can be phased out in favor of a cue or cues that have been reinforced during the training sessions. As a result, your dog will immediately respond by reacting, obeying, and performing actions to your hand gestures or verbal commands. Watching this unfold is a highly satisfying process, which empowers your friend to be the best he can, and while you have fulfilled your role as *alpha* and pack leader.

Why is clicking effective over using a word cue first?

The clicking sound is a unique sound that is not found in nature, and it is more precise than a verbal command. Verbal commands can be confusing because the human voice has many tonal variations, where as the clicker consistently makes a sound that your dog will not confuse with any other noise. It is also effective because it is directed at him and followed by good things. Therefore, your dog completely understands which action is desired and your dog will quickly understand that the click is followed by a reward.

The clicker sound is produced in a quick and accurate way that is in response to the slightest actions that your dog makes. This clarity of function of this tool increases the bond between you and your dog, as a result making your dog more interested in the training sessions, and ultimately your relationship more engaging and entertaining. Dare I say fun? On that note, do not forget to always have fun and add variety to your training sessions. Variety is the spice of life, mix up those treats, rewards, and commands.

Clicker training works this way

At the *exact* instant the action occurs, the trainer clicks. If a dog begins to *sit*, the trainer recognizes that, and *at the exact moment the dog's buttocks hits the ground the trainer clicks and offers the dog a reward.* Usually the reward is a small kernel sized food treat, but a reward can be a toy, play, or affection. Whatever the dog enjoys is a reward worth giving.

In as soon as 2-3 clicks have been issued a dog will associate the sound of the click with something it enjoys. Once the association is made, it will repeat the action it did when hearing the click. Click = Reward. When this goes off in the dog's head, repeating the action makes sense.

The three steps are as follows:

1. *Get the action* you request

2. *Mark the action* with your clicker

3. *Reinforce the action* with a reward

How do you ask for actions when clicker training your dog?

During clicker training before adding a cue command such as "stay," you wait until your dog completely understands the action. A cue is the name of the action or it can be a hand signal that you are using when you ask your dog to perform a specific action. Your dog should know the action *stay* from the click and reward before you verbally name it. *He or she has connected being still to receiving a click and reward.*

When training you do not want to add the *cue* until your dog has been clicked 5-10 times for the action, and is accurately responding in a manner that clearly shows he understands which action earns the click and reward. This is called introducing the cue.

Teaching your dog the name of the cue or action requires saying or signaling before your dog repeats the action. After several repetitions, begin to click and reward when your dog performs the action, be sure the cue is given before the reward. Your dog will learn to listen and watch for the cue, knowing that if he does the action a reward will follow.

Clicker Training Help

If your dog is not obeying the cue, answer the following questions and then revise your training process so that your dog knows the meaning of the clicker sound cue during all situations. Importantly, be sure that your dog is and feels rewarded for doing the correct action.

Trainers never assume the dog is intentionally disobeying without asking the questions below.

1. Does your dog understand the meaning of the cue?

2. Does your dog understand the meaning of the cue in the situation first taught, but *not* in the different situations that you gave the cue?

3. Is the *reward* for doing the action you want, satisfying your dog's needs? Is the treat or toy worth the effort?

Once you have answered these questions, change your training process to be certain that your dog understands the clicker/cue in all situations, including high distraction situations such as at a busy park. Then be sure your dog is adequately rewarded and that it is clear your dog feels that he or she has been properly rewarded. This will help put you two back on the path of mutual understanding during your training sessions.

~ Paws On – Paws Off ~

Let's Talk Treats

You are training your puppy and he is doing well, *of course*, because he is the best dog in the world! *Oh yes he is.* Because of this fact, you want to make sure that you are giving your dog the right kind of treats. Treats are easy. As long as you stay away from the things that aren't good for dogs, such as; avocado, onions, garlic, coffee, tea, caffeinated drinks, grapes, raisins, macadamia nuts, peaches, plums, pits, seeds, persimmons, chocolate, whiskey & soda, Guinness Stout, just to name a few.

You can make treats from many different foods. First, treats should be small, kernel sized, and easy to grab from a pocket or concealable container (treat pouches are available). When you are outdoors and there are many distractions, treats should be of a higher quality and coveted by your pooch, we call it a higher value treat because it is worthy of your dog breaking away from the activity he is engaged. Perhaps cubes of cheese, dried meat, special kibble or the neighbor cat (just joking all you cat lovers). Make sure you mix it up and keep a variety of snacks available when you are out and about. Nothing is worse during treat training than your dog or puppy turning his nose up at a treat because he has grown bored of it or it holds a lesser value than something else does that currently interests him.

Here are some treat ideas:

- No sugar, whole grain cereals are good. Cheerios are good choice. There is no need for milk, bowl, or a spoon. You can just give your dog the goods, as is.

- Kibble (dry foods). Put some in a paper bag and boost the aroma factor by tossing in some bacon or another meat product. Dogs are all about those yummy smell sensations.

- Beef Jerky that preferably has no pepper or heavy seasoning.

- Carrot, apple pieces, and some dogs even enjoy melons.

- Baby food meat products. You know the ones, those strange little suspect pink sausage things.

- Commercial dog treats. Be careful, there as there are tons of them on the market. Look for those that do not have preservatives, by products, or artificial colors.

- Cubed meats that are preferably not highly processed or salted.

- Shredded cheese, string cheese or cubed cheese. Dogs love cheese!

- Cream cheese, peanut butter, or spray cheese. Give your dog a small dollop to lick for every proper behavior.

- Ice Cube, Not the rap star but the frozen water treats. Your dog will love crunching these up. . If your dog has dental problems, proceed cautiously.

Avoid feeding your hairy friend from the dining table; because you do not want to teach your dog to beg when people are sitting down to eat. When treating, give treats far from the dinner table or a good distance from where people normally gather to eat.

Giving Treats

Treats, treats, *treats!* *"Come and get 'em."* How many times have you heard a friend or family member tell you about some crazy food that their dog loves? Dogs do love a massive variety of foods; unfortunately, not all of the foods that they think they want to eat are good for them. Dog treating is not rocket science but it does take a little research, common sense, and paying attention to how your dog reacts after wolfing down a treat.

I am going to throw out some ideas for treats for training as well as some regular ole "Good Dog" treats for your sidekick and friend in mischief. I will touch on the proper time to treat, the act of giving the treat, types of treats, and bribery vs. reward.

Types of Treats

Love and attention is considered a reward and is certainly a positive reinforcement that can be just as effective as an edible treat. Dog treating is comprised of edibles, praise, love, and attention. Engaging in play or allowing some quality time with their favorite piece of rawhide is also effectual. At times, these treats are crucial to dog training.

Human foods that are safe for dogs, include most fruits and veggies, cut up meats that are raw or cooked, yogurt,

29

peanut butter, kibble, and whatever else you discover that your dog likes, but be sure that it is good for him, in particular his digestive system. Remember, not all human foods are good for dogs. Please read up on the dos and don'ts regarding human foods and dogs. A "treat" is considered something about the size of a kernel of corn. All a dog needs is a little taste to keep him interested. The *kernel size* is something that is swiftly eaten and swallowed, making it non-distracting from training. Remember, a treat is just quick tasted, used for enticement and reinforcement.

Giving the Treat

Try to avoid treating your dog when he is over stimulated and running amuck in an unfocused state of mind. This can be counterproductive and might reinforce a negative behavior resulting in you not being able to get your dog's attention.

When giving the treat, allow your dog to get a big doggie whiff of that nibble of tasty food treat, but keep it up and away from a possible attempt at a quick snatch and grab. Due to their keen sense of smell, they will know long before you would that there is a tasty snack nearby. Issue your command and wait for him to obey before presenting the doggie reward. Remember when dog treating, it is important to be patient and loving, but it is equally important not to give the treat until he obeys. Try to use treating to reward the kickback mellow dog, not the out of control or over-excited dog.

Some dogs have a natural gentleness to them and always take from your hand gently, while other dogs need some guidance to achieve this. If your dog is a bit rough during treat grabbing, go ahead and train the command "gentle!"

when giving treats. Be firm from this point forward. Give up no treats unless taken gently. Remain steadfast with your decision to implement this, and soon your pup or dog will comply, if he wants the tasty treat.

Time to Treat

The best time to be issuing dog treats is in between his or her meals. During training, always keep the tastiest treat in reserve in case you need to reel in your dog's attention back to the current training session. It is good to keep in mind that treating too close to meal times makes all treats less effective, so remember this when planning your training sessions. Obviously, if your dog is full from mealtime he will be less likely to want a treat reward than if he is a bit hungry, therefore your training session will likely be more difficult and far less effective.

What's In the Treats?

Before purchasing, look at the ingredients on the treat packaging, and make certain there are no chemicals, fillers, additives, colors and things that are unhealthy. Certain human foods that are tasty to us might not be so tasty to your dog, and he will tell you. Almost all dogs love some type of raw or cooked meats. In tiny nibble sizes, these treats work great to get their attention where you want it focused.

Many people like to make homemade treats and that is fine, just keep to the rules we just mentioned and watch what you are adding while you are having fun in the kitchen. Remember to research and read the list of vegetables dogs can and cannot eat, and note that pits and seeds can cause choking and intestinal issues, such as dreaded doggy flatulence. Remove the seeds and pits, and clean all fruits and veggies before slicing it into doggie size treats.

Bribery vs. Reward Dog Treating

The other day a friend of mine mentioned *bribery* for an action when he wanted his dog to shake his hand. I thought about it later and thought I would clarify for my readers. *Bribery* is the act of offering the food in advance to get the dog to act out a command or behavior. *Reward* is giving your dog his favorite toy, food, love, affection *after* he has performed the behavior.

An example of bribery would be, if you want your dog to come and you hold out in front of you in your hand a huge slab of steak before calling him. Reward would be giving your dog the steak after he obeyed the "come!" command.

Bribed dogs learn to comply with your wishes only when they *see* food. The rewarded dog realizes that he only gets his reward after performing the desired action. This also assists by introducing non-food items as rewards when training and treating. Rewards such as play, toys, affection, and praise can be substituted for treats.

~ Paws On – Paws Off ~

Characteristic Herding Breed Traits

Herding dogs were originally bred for working or herding stock. They are referred to as working, stock, or herding dogs. The characteristics of this breed features heightened herding instincts derived from ancient hunting capabilities. Early in human history, dogs and humans began living and working with one another, relying on each other for survival. Humans began developing the herding breeds to manage domesticated animals, while simultaneously developing other breeds as guardians to protect the flocks from all types of predators. Herding and guarding dogs work together to keep the livestock together and safe. For example, the Great Pyrenees Mountain Dogs steadfastly handles the guarding duties while the Pyrenean Shepherds diligently take care of the herding duties. Herders are known for their abilities to obey vocal and whistle commands, as well as think and act independently while performing their jobs.

Depending upon the different recognitions and classifications, I uncovered eight-eight herding breeds in the world. The Herding Group is made up of sheep and cattle dogs that were, and are still bred to round up livestock and retrieve all stragglers. Herding dogs use a variety of techniques, such as nipping, barking, running, and engaging in intense eye contact with their animal charges. Australian Kelpies and Koolies are known to run atop sheep (backing sheep) to move them along, and Border Collies are known for their staring and crouching style that enables them to mesmerize and herd almost any animal. Australian Cattle Dogs (Blue/Red Heelers) will nip at heels, or if necessary jump up to nip under a cows neck. Fearless, intelligent, alert, independent, and blessed with stamina and intense energy levels, these herding breeds possess the natural traits necessary to accomplish their jobs proficiently. Beyond their herding abilities, some in this group are used as police, guide, and therapy dogs.

Versatility allows many of these breeds to herd cattle, ducks, geese, sheep, and goats.

Additionally, they will herd children, household pets, other dogs, and if not tethered they will even attempt to round up motor vehicles. Because of their natural instincts, herding breeds that do not have a job and are to be household pets will need to be vigorously exercised and given opportunities to complete tasks. This can be accomplished through agility training, tracking games, herding trials, daily accompaniment with their humans on bike rides, jogs, hikes, runs, brisk walks, or anything that will help deplete their seemingly endless energy reserves. A herder that is not having their exercise needs met can become destructive, aggressive, or display other negative behaviors. Before bringing home a herding dog, you must be certain that you can provide the proper amount of exercise and stimulation for these breeds. Most herding breeds need a few exercise outings per day, which should include a minimum of two hours of rigorous exercise.

Herding dogs come in a variety of coat types, heights, and weights. For example, the little Corgi's stand only 10 - 12 inches (25 - 30 cm) tall, while the French Beauceron stands 26–28 in (66–71 cm) tall. Most herders reside in the medium to large size classification. Amazingly, the little Corgi's are wonderfully efficient herding dogs that have been around since the Vikings brought them to Wales almost two thousand years ago. Since at least the 10th century, the little Pembroke Welsh Corgi has been herding cattle, ducks, geese, horses, and sheep. In recent times, herding dogs have been employed to keep ducks and geese clear of golf courses and airports.

Many in this group tend to be wary of strangers, but form tight loyal bonds with their handlers and family. They make a great addition as a family companion and enjoy being in the company of their humans. Nipping is something that needs to be addressed early when they are puppies. Always supervise your dog around small children. When children are running around playing, your herding dog immediately recognizes this as a herd to be tended, and they will begin nipping at the children's heels. You can sometimes observe them instinctually circling a group of children, in classic herding behavior. They do not intend to do harm, but a nip can be painful and should not be allowed. Early and ongoing socialization will help with aggression, possessiveness, territorialism, and other potential negative behaviors that can surface. Herders are happiest when they have a purpose. These are some of the most intelligent and active dog breeds, and they have a strong predisposition for work.

The AKC created The Herding Group in 1983, and it is the newest American Kennel Club classification. Before the creation of their own group, these breeds were classified in the Working Group. In fact, this group has some of the most intelligent of all dog breeds. The Border Collie has been ranked as one of the most intelligent. Other herding breeds ranked inside the top ten of some lists include the Australian Cattle Dog, German Shepherd, Shetland Sheepdog (Sheltie), and the Rottweiler.

Training

Now you are probably wondering, "how the heck do I go about training my herding breed?" First off, you need to be dedicated, consistent, focused, and firm. In your favor, most of these breeds are intelligent and eager to learn. Additionally, they respond well to positive training methods such as clicker training. Remember to keep your dog well exercised at all times. To help increase focus and attention, provide your dog with ample exercise prior to the training sessions. If you are using treats in your sessions, train prior to meal times so that your dog is hungry and the treat will keep their attention. Find quiet, low distraction areas to begin your training sessions. Later, you can take the training outdoors and then gradually increase the distraction level. Many herding dogs are easy to work with during training because of their willingness to learn and perform. Herders can also be trained to become very good watchdogs.

There are many negative behaviors that may manifest with the herding breeds, and should be addressed early, such as nipping, bumping, jumping-up, aggression towards other animals and humans, challenging authority, leash pulling, protectiveness, agitation during car rides, digging, excessive attention seeking, and chasing.

To satisfy their mental and physical needs, keep a regular schedule. Firm and consistent training can shape your dog's behavior to be in compliance with the rules of etiquette that you have clearly laid out. Herders are naturally athletic and they adore dog sports, excelling in agility, herding, tracking, and much more.

When using treats while training your herder, pay close attention and take note of which treats your dog covets most. Utilize these favorites in your training sessions. As said before, be sure to train your dog before meals so that he or she is at their hungriest. Initially, keep the training sessions very short, at around five to ten minutes each. You can extend to longer sessions if you realize that you can hold your herder's attention longer. Keep the sessions short while your herder is a puppy.

Training Tips

- Train your dog after exercise – Before training take your dog on a brisk walk to get rid of any built up energy.

- Get to know your herder's motivations and favorite rewards, such as praise, fetch, sport, or play, so that during and after each training session you can provide what they love.

- Train your dog before meals – Make sure your dog is hungry as this makes food rewards better motivators. Also, use verbal praise and affection as rewards.

- Have fun! Always bringing your sense of humor and patience to the sessions. Use a variety of treats and requests.

- Do not train if you are tired or in a bad mood – Your dog will notice this and neither of you will benefit.

- Only reward success, never failure – Keep a positive attitude, reward successes, ignore failures.

- Keep it short – About 10 minutes.

- Always end on a high note - End with a successful compliance while using a happy vocal tone and praise. If necessary, provide your dog with an easy request so that you can end the session on a high note.

Examples of mentally stimulating activities for your herding dog

- *Retrieval games are physically and mentally stimulating.*

- *Agility games that are physical, but primarily mental, you can turn your household items into a course.*

-*Tracking, this uses dog's natural scenting abilities to find hidden objects.*

- *Herding trials or tests allow dogs to use their natural or trained herding abilities.*

- *Free play with other familiar dogs assists in socialization, energy release, and stimulation.*

- *Trick performance that is rewarded with access to your dogs highly valued items.*

- *Obedience classes.*

- *Flyball for physical activity.*

- *Hide and Seek with family members is good physical exercise for all.*

- Working livestock is both mentally and physically challenging for dogs.

- Treibball is a relatively new dog sport where dogs gather and move large balls that represent a flock of animals.

I am confident that you will enjoy the unique personalities and abilities of whichever breed that you choose to bring home.

Enjoy your herding breed!

PART II BEGIN SCHOOL

Clicker Response Training

Important - *Conceal the treat! <u>Do not</u> show your puppy the treat before pressing the clicker* and it making the clicking sound. If you do this, your puppy will be responding to the treat and not the click. This will undermine your training strategy.

Here is how you begin training. Start by observing your puppy. You are looking for a good behavior to reward or just that your puppy is not doing anything considered as a bad behavior. What we are doing here is training your puppy to associate the clicker with doing something good. As long as your puppy is relaxed and not doing anything bad, you can begin to train this clicker response training. The result will be that whenever you click, your puppy will know that it is for being a good or an obedient puppy and that he or she has a reward coming.

Timing is crucial for training your puppy. The methods you will be using to train your puppy to respond to the clicker are by immediately clicking the correct action, followed by treating your puppy. It does not take long for your puppy to realize that hearing the clicker means that he or she will be receiving a treat. Make sure that the treat is easily available and immediately follows the clicking sound.

Please be aware that throughout this training guide, *Click and Treat is sometimes written as C/T.* For writing sake, I also refer to your dog as male even though I know many people have female dogs, no offence meant.

Crucial – *Never click without treating, and never treat without clicking. This maintains the connection between clicking and treating.*

Steps

1. When your puppy is relaxed, stand, or kneel down about an arm's reach away from your puppy. Click and give your puppy a treat from your treat pouch.

2. Repeat clicking and treating about 5-15 times. Pause a few seconds between clicks to allow your puppy to resume what he was doing. Do not click and treat if he seems to be begging for another treat. Find times throughout the day when he is acting a good behavior. This teaches your puppy to associate the click with good things, which in this case is a food treat.

3. When you click and your puppy's head swings around in anticipation of a treat, then you know that your puppy has made the association between the clicking sound and a reward.

4. Repeat steps one and two the next day. When your puppy is quickly responding to the click, then you can begin training commands.

Teaching puppies to respond to this method can take several training sessions, but in many cases after a dozen or less click and treats, puppies begin to connect the clicking sound with a treat. At the end of a 5-minute session, puppies tend to swing their head around when they hear the clicker sound.

HELPFUL HINT: After some time passes, puppies tend to stop in their tracks and instantly come to you for a treat. DO NOT use this as an excuse to use the clicker to get your dog to *come* to you.

Name Recognition

Now we are going to teach your puppy some specific things. Let us start with a base exercise of getting your puppy to respond to his or her *name*. I assume that you have gone through the painstaking process and named your puppy, now you want him or her to learn his or her name. This can be easy and fun.

Now that your puppy responds to the clicker and knows that treats come with the clicking sound, you can begin teaching him commands and tricks. Name recognition is the perfect place to start. Teaching your puppy his name is basic, but it is necessary to have your puppy's attention so that you can teach other tricks, gain his attention, and direct him. Below, I used my dog Axel's name.

- Gather a nice variety of treats and put them in your pockets, treat pouch, or on a tabletop out of sight and your puppy's reach.

1. Ignore your puppy until he looks directly at you, when he does, *click and treat* him. Repeat 10-15 times. This teaches your puppy to associate the click with a treat when he looks your way.

2. Next, when your puppy looks at you, begin adding your puppy's name right before you *click and treat*, say, "Axel," and C/T.

3. Continue doing this until your puppy will look at you when you say his or her name.

4. Gradually phase out clicking and treating your puppy every time that he or she looks at you. For example, do not C/T one out of two times, then one out of three, four, and then not at all. Do not decrease too quickly. Occasionally you should C/T to refresh your puppy's memory and association that good things come from responding to his name. Observe your puppy's abilities and pace. The goal is that your puppy will obey all the commands without a reward, and only by a vocal or physical cue.

Responding to his or her name is the most important behavior because it is will form the base of all the other things that you will be teaching your puppy later. Therefore, you will want to spend the time and give this a considerable amount of attention. Repeat the exercise all around the house, while he is on the leash outside in the back and front yards, down the street, or in the park. Make sure that you practice this while there are distractions, such as when there are guests present, his favorite toys are visible, there is food around, and when he is among other dogs. Call your puppy's name then C/T while maintaining good *eye contact*. Keep on practicing until there is no doubt that when you speak your puppy's name, he or she knows that is they.

Name recognition will avoid trouble later on down the line. For example, if your puppy gets into something that he should not, such as a scrap with another dog, chasing a cat, squirrel, or a time-share pyramid scheme, you can call your puppy's name to gain his attention, say "come" and he will come for the treat. You want your puppy to come no matter what, so training come is a crucial command to teach and regularly practice for the lifetime of your puppy.

After time and practice, he will eventually come only because you command it. Your puppy needs to know his or her name so that you can teach your puppy other commands.

- It may sound odd, but also try doing this when you are in different physical positions, such as sitting, standing, and lying down. Mix it up so that he gets used to hearing his name in a variety of areas and situations. Repeat this process throughout the different areas of your house, and both the front and backyards. No matter the situation, this command must be obeyed.

Before moving forward be certain that your puppy knows and responds to his name being called. Continue this into adulthood to be certain that you are able to grab your puppy's attention during any circumstance. If your puppy is responding to his or her name, move forward to the "come" command.

~ Paws On – Paws Off ~

"Come" Absolutely Essential

After your puppy recognizes and begins responding to his name being called, then the "come!" command is the one that you want to teach next. *Why?* Because this one could save his life, save your sanity, and save you running through the neighborhood in the middle of the night wearing little more than a robe and slippers.

If by chance he is checking out the olfactory magic of the trash bin, the best way to redirect your dog is to yell, *"come!"* followed by an immediate reward when he does. Petting, verbal praise, or play is an appropriate reinforcement incentive for this type of situation.

An option is to use your own special verbal cue command that will grab your dog's attention no matter what he is engaged in. The word *come* can be spoken regularly during a telephone call or in a conversation, but some words are rarely spoken and thus your dog will better recognize the word as being unique. You can pick a unique cue command that is your own special command. "Axel Cactus," or "Axel Jax," is two examples instead of "Axel come" or "Axel here." When your dog hears this special cue word, such as "Axel cactus," he will recognize the special command and he will associate it with a special supersized treat. Using a word that you can say easily and only has one or two syllables will make it easier for you and your dog. Only substitute this special word if you find it easy and natural to speak, because it will be difficult to change the "come" command cue word later.

Here's what to do-

- If you picked a unique command, begin here. We will not use the clicker. Grab your assortment of treats such as steak, bacon, kibble, cheese, or whatever treats your dog covets most. Start with the tastiest treat in hand. If you have picked a unique cue command that is your own special command, when your dog hears this word, he will associate it with a special treat. For example, say the words "Axel cactus," and give him a piece of treat-sized steak. Keep repeating and mix up the treats between kibble, steak, bacon, and remember to add praise. Do ten repetitions then proceed onto the next step.

- Think *treats*. Find a quiet, low distraction place so that both of you can focus. Place a treat on the floor and walk to the other side of the room. Next, hold out a hand with a visible treat in it. Now, say your dog's name to get his attention, followed by the command "come." Use a pleasant, happy tone when you do this. When your dog begins to move towards you, press the clicker, and begin to praise him all the way to the treat in your hand. The object is for him to avoid the treat on the ground and come to you. When he gets to you, *treat* him from your hand and offer a "good boy or girl." You have already clicked so do not click again, only give the treat. Do this 10-12 times and then take a break. Only treat your dog if he comes all the way to you.

- For the next session, you can request the assistance of a family member and have them stand at a distance (5-6 paces) opposite you, place the treat on the floor, and then take turns calling your dog back and forth between the two of you. Treat your dog each time he comes all of the way to either of you. Do this a dozen times. The object is to reinforce to your dog the idea that coming to his name is not only for you, but is beneficial to him as well.

- This time, grab your clicker. As before, put a treat on the ground, move across the room, and then call his name to get his attention. This time, hold out an empty hand and give the command. This will mess with him a little, but that is okay. As soon as he starts to come to you, give him praise and when he reaches you *click and treat* from your pouch. If your dog is not coming all of the way to you, as your dog begins to come press the clicker, and when he gets to you the first time, give him a supersize treat serving (7-10 treats) using the opposite hand you were luring with. After the first time he comes to you, each additional time your dog comes all of the way to you, reward your dog with a regular sized treat serving. Do this about a dozen times and then take a break.

- Keep practicing this with an empty hand and this training will eventually become a hand signal. This may be trained over several sessions and days. You then want to take this another step by fading out the hand signal and only using a verbal cue without treating each time. Begin gradually reducing treating by only treating one out of two times, one out three times, then one out of four, five, six, and finally none.

Occasionally treat to reinforce the worth of your dog coming to you upon command. Make sure your dog is coming on command with each cue, and that your dog will eventually *come* when commanded by all family members and friends. By the end of this section, you and your dog should have the hand signal and verbal command that your dog responds to when you command, "come" or your special cue word.

Let's get complex

- Now, we begin to make it more difficult on your dog. We begin adding distractions. Start with a treat in hand, and then fade the exercise to using only the verbal command. At first, the treat will be the lure for your dog to follow, but the goal is to dispense with it and only use the vocal command.

Indoors and outdoors, practice when distractions are present, such as other animals, children, noises, or adults are present. Keep a log of how your dog is progressing with different amount of distractions.

Indoors, this is an example of what increasingly more distracting situations could be; you begin indoors with a toy in your hand, then when another person is present, and then both. Then both a person is in the room and the television is on, followed by the doorbell ringing. Then move to calling your dog from different rooms of the house and gradually introduce other distractions such as the stereo is on while other people are in the room at the same time.

This is an example of increasing outdoor distraction. Practice calling "come" when you and your dog are in the backyard with another animal or person, then a person and animal together, then multiple people conversing while children are running around, and then toys or balls are being thrown. Eventually, move out into the streets and into a busy location. Keep track of your dog's progress as the situations become more and more distracting. You want your dog to come every time you call "Axel come," no matter how much noise and movement is happening around him.

If your dog begins coming upon command seven or eight times out of ten in each situation, this shows that the two of you are making very good progress on your way to nine out of ten times that your dog comes to you no matter what distractions are happening around him.

We all want that dog and I want you to have that dog that is six houses away, but the second you call his name and command "come," he comes running towards you no matter what he is engaged in.

Interrupting Fetch Exercises, Hide & Seek, and The Decoy Exercise

Increasing the difficulty now, remember to always train in a safe area. Practice all of these with increasing distractions, and both indoors and outdoors. Only practice one of these per session, and then begin mixing up the order of the exercises.

- Interrupting Fetch Exercises

Get a good-sized handful of your dog's favorite treat. Then, lob a ball or a piece of food. As your dog is in the process of chasing it, call him by name. If he comes *after* he gets the ball/food, give your dog a little reward of one piece of treat. If he comes *before* he gets the ball/food, give your dog a supersized (7-10) serving of treats.

If your dog is not responding, throw the ball and quickly place a treat to his nose, when he comes to you click and supersize treat your dog. Then begin fading using a treat lure.

After you have thrown the ball/food a few times, it is time to change it up. Now, fake throwing something and call your dog. If your dog goes looking for the ball/food before he comes to you, give a small treat. If he comes immediately, give the supersized treat portion. Repeat 7-10 times.

- Hide & Seek

While you are outside, and your dog is distracted and does not seem to know you exist, quickly *hide*. When your dog comes looking for you, and finds you, *click and treat* your dog with lots of love and praise. By adding a little drama, make it seem like an extremely big deal that your dog has found you. This is something that you can regularly practice and reward.

- The Decoy

One person calls the dog; we will call this person the *trainer*. One person tries to distract the dog with food and toys; we will call this person the *decoy*. After your dog is called, if the dog goes toward the decoy, the decoy person should turn away from the dog and neither of you offer rewards. When the dog goes towards the trainer, he should be rewarded by both the trainer and the decoy. Repeat 7-10 times.

HELPFUL HINTS

- Let your dog know that his coming to you is always the best thing ever, sometimes offering supersized treat rewards. Always reward by treating or praising, and when appropriate you can add play with a favorite toy or ball.

- Never, call your Beardie for something he might find unpleasant. If you are leaving the field where he has been running, call your dog, put on the leash, and play a little more. This will pacify and distract from any negative association with coming to you.

- You are calling, and your puppy is not responding. What do you do now? Try running backwards away from your dog, crouch, and clap, and then show your dog a toy or food. When he comes, still reward him even though he stressed you out. *Running towards your dog signals to play catch me, so avoid doing this.*

- If your dog has been off the lead for a while, remember to give him a C/T when he checks in with you.

- You should practice "come!" five to ten times daily, forever. It is one of those potentially life-saving commands and helps with all daily activities and interactions. The goal is that your dog will come running whether you are in or out of sight and from any audible distance.

~ Paws On – Paws Off ~

"Drop it" A Must Learn

Teaching your Beardie to *drop it* is very important. Why you wonder? Well, if you have young puppy, you know that it is one giant mouth that everything goes into. Sometimes valuable and dangerous things go into that mouth. Rumor has it that Stephen Hawking actually got the idea of the black hole from his puppy's ever-consuming mouth.

If you teach your dog correctly, when you give the command "drop it!" he will open his mouth and drop whatever is in there, and most importantly, he will allow you to retrieve it. When teaching the *drop it* command you must make a good trade for what your dog has in his mouth. You need to, *out treat* your dog by offering better treat of higher value than what he has in his mouth. In addition, it is a good idea to stay calm and not to chase your puppy.

If you teach this command well, your puppy will eventually enjoy hearing the drop it commands. This command will also build trust. If you say, "drop it," then you retrieve the item, and afterwards treat your dog, your dog will know that you are not there to steal the things he finds and enjoys. Because of the trust that will develop, he will *not guard* his favorite toys or food. Guarding is a negative behavior that can be avoided through proper socialization and acts such as in this training.

Teach "Drop It!" Like This

- Gather good treats, the top-notch stuff, and a few items your dog might like to chew on; toys, rawhide, or your dogs favorite. With treats in hand, encourage your dog to chew on one of the items. When it is in his mouth, *put the treat close to his nose* and say, "drop it!" As soon as he opens his mouth, *click and treat* him as you pick up the item. Then return the item to your dog. Now, your dog may not want to chew the item because there are treats in the area and want his mouth free for those treats. That is fine, stop training and keep the treats handy, and throughout the day when you see him pick something up, practice the *drop it* command. Do this at least ten times per day.

In the event that he picks up a forbidden item, like Uncle Clumpy's wooden leg, you may not want to give it back to him; that is fine, but when you take the leg away, remember to give your puppy an extra tasty treat, or supersized serving. You want your puppy to know he has been properly rewarded.

- Once you have done this treat to the nose *drop it* command ten times, try t without holding the treat to his nose. Continue to use your hand but it will be empty. Say the command, and when he drops the item, C/T, and give him a treat from your pocket or pouch. Make sure that the first time he drops it without holding a treat to his nose that you give him a supersized treat serving. Practice this over a few days and train ng sessions. Do not rush forward to the next step.

- Moving forward, now give your dog something more special, like a hard chew pig ear, rawhide or that special thing that makes your dog salivate. Next, hold this new chewy in your hand and cffer it to your dog but *do not let it go*. When your dog has the chewy in his mouth, say the "drop it" command. When your dog drops it, C/T, give your dog extra treats the first time he drops it and then again offer the chew back to him.

Again, because better treats are available, he may not take the chewy back. This is a good sign, but indicates a time for a break. Later, return to the training and repeat it about a dozen times before you move on to the next phase of "drop it!" If your dog is not dropping it after clicking, use a higher value treat.

- Now, repeat the exercise above, but this time do not hold onto the chew, just let him have it. As soon as your dog has it in his mouth, give the command "drop it!" When your dog drops the chewy, C/T a supersized portion, *and* give the chew back to him to keep. Your dog will be thrilled.

During this exercise, if your dog does not drop the chewy, if necessary show the treat first, and then work up to having him drop it before the treat appears. This in actuality is *bribery*, and I do not suggest doing this type of intervention on a regular basis, nor do I suggest utilizing this action elsewhere during training. *Warning*, use this method as a last resort, not as a short cut and discontinue quickly.

Once you have done this a dozen times successfully move onto the next step.

- Try the command with the things around the house that he is not supposed to chew on, such as pens, chip bags, socks, gloves, tissues, your shoes, and that 15th century Guttenberg bible.

Then, try this exercise outside where there are plenty of distractions. Be sure and gather up the best treats when working outside, and keep moving into further distracting situations. Your goal is to have the *drop it* commands obeyed in any situation full of distractions.

- Try the command "drop it," when playing fetch, and other games. When your dog returns to you with his ball, command, "drop it," and when he does offer up the praise and or a treat.

- Gradually phase out clicking and treating your dog every time that on command he drops something. Begin gradually reducing treating by only treating one out of two times, one out three times, then one out of four, five, six, and finally none. Do not decrease too quickly. Observe your dog's abilities and pace. The goal is that your dog will obey all the commands without a reward, and only by a vocal or physical cue.

Know These Things-

- If your puppy already likes to grab things and have you chase him, start by teaching your dog that you will *not* go chasing him. If your dog grabs and runs, ignore him. He will get bored and drop the item on his own. *Remember that ignoring means sight, sound, and body language.*

- If your dog will not drop an item, you can manually retrieve the item by placing your fingers on the lips of your dog's upper jaw. Attempt to calm your dog beforehand. Place your hand over the top of your dogs muzzle; apply even pressure on the upper lips by using your index and thumb fingers and pressing inwards into his teeth. In most cases, your dog will open its mouth to avoid having his lips pinched, and then you can retrieve the item in question, which might be a dead bird, dried dog poop, or an antibiotic. This may take a couple of practices to get the pressure and spot correct. If all fails you can use both hands and try to separate the jaw by pulling, *not jerking*, the upper and lower jaw apart.

-You can try distracting your puppy's attention by knocking on wood, or the door, as if it is a knock at the door. Often a puppy will want to investigate and thus drop whatever is in their mouth.

~ Paws On – Paws Off ~

Let's Sit

Sitting is one of the basic commands that you will use regularly during life with your dog. Teaching your Beardie to *sit* establishes human leadership by shaping your dog to understand who the boss is, and it will be a perfect substitute command for other problem behaviors such as jumping up on people, and for the polite etiquette of patiently waiting for you, the trusted leader. Teaching your dog to sit is easy too, and a great way for you to work on all the alpha things touched upon thus far.

- Find a quiet place and get your treats together. Wait until your puppy sits down by his own will. As soon as his fuzzy rump hits the floor, *click and treat*. Feed your pup while he is still sitting and then get him up and standing again. Continue doing this until your pup is sitting back down right away after you have clicked and treated him for sitting.

- Now, say, "sit" and as he begins to sit, then C/T. From here on, only treat your pup when he sits after being commanded to do so.

Try these variations for better sitting behavior:

- Practice five minutes a day in places with increasingly more distractions. Continue adding people, animals, and noises to the training sessions. As with come, you want your dog to sit during any situation.

- Run around with your dog, play with a toy, get him worked up a bit, and then ask your dog to sit. Click and treat your dog well when he does.

- Ask your dog to sit before you give him stuff that he likes, such as going outside, food, toys, verbal praise, getting into the car, and petting. Having your dog sit before setting his food bowl down is something you can practice every day forever.

- Command your dog to sit in a variety of situations, such as when strangers are around, when there is food on the table, outdoors, barbequing, in the park, before putting his or her food bowl down, before opening doors, and so forth. Keep practicing in all situations you encounter and continue gradually increasing the distractions in which you command, "sit," and your dog complies. Sit is a powerful command, and it will be useful for the life of your dog. Later add "sit-stay" to keep your dog in place until you release him or her.

-Gradually phase out clicking and treating your dog every time that on command he obeys the "sit" command. Begin gradually reducing treating by only treating one out of two times, one out three times, then one out of four, five, six, and finally none. Do not decrease too quickly. Observe your dog's abilities and pace. The goal is that your dog will obey all the commands without a reward, and only by a vocal or physical cue.

- Multiple times a day you can practice the sit command whenever the situation is appropriate.

~ Paws On – Paws Off ~

"Leave it" Important for Living

"Leave it" is a different command than "drop it!" The goal of the "leave it" command is to get your dog's attention away from any object *before* it is in your dog's mouth. This will keep him safe from dangerous objects, such as chemicals, dropped medications, glass, wires, oily rags, or that ceramic sculpture you are working on. Not to mention all of the icky things dogs love to bring to their humans. You can teach the "leave it" command as soon as your dog recognizes his own name.

- Start with a treat in each fisted hand. Let him have a sniff of one of your fists. When he eventually looks away from the fist and has stopped trying to get the treat, *click and treat*, but treat your dog from the *other* hand than he sniffed. Repeat this exercise until he refrains from trying to get the treat from your fist.

- Now, open your hand with the treat in it and then show him. Close your hand if he tries to get the treat. Do this until he simply ignores the treat in the open hand, known as the decoy hand. When he ignores it, click and give your dog the treat from the *other* hand. Keep doing this until he ignores the treat in the open hand from the start of the exercise. When you have reached this point, add the command "leave it." Now, open the decoy hand, say "leave it" just once for each repetition, and when your dog does, click and treat him from the other hand.

- Now put the treat on the floor and say, "leave it." Cover it with your hand if he tries to get it. When your dog looks away from the treat that is lying on the floor, *click and treat* your dog from the other hand that is not covering the treat. Continue issuing the command "leave it" until your dog does not try to get the treat that is on the floor.

- Now, try the following steps.

Put the treat on the floor, and say, "leave it" and then you stand up. Click and treat if he obeys. Now, walk your dog by the treat while on his leash, and say, "leave it." If he goes for it, prevent him from getting it by restraining him with the leash. C/T him when he ignores the treat. Increase the length of time between the "leave it" command and the treat. Teaching your dog to leave it with a treat first will allow you to build up to objects such as toys, animals, sugary liquids, pills, spills, and people. You can build up to more and more difficult items with ease once he gets the idea in his head that *leave it*, means good rewards for him. Begin with a low value item such as dropping a piece of kibble, then move to a piece of tasty meat, toys, animals, people, etc.

- After your dog is successful at leaving the treat and other items, take the training outside into the yard, then gradually add people, animals, and other distractions. Next, head to the Dog Park, or local store down the street, and then other places with increasing distractions.

Remember to keep your puppy clear of dog parks until at least after seven to ten weeks and after his first round of vaccines. Some suggest waiting until after a dog's second round of vaccinations.

Continue practicing daily until your dog has it down pat. This is another potential life saving command that you will use regularly during living with your dog.

- At this point, you can have some real fun. You can place a dog biscuit on your pups paw, snout, or head and say "leave it." Gradually increase the time that your pup must leave the biscuit alone. Try this when your pup is in the sitting and down positions. Have some fun and be sure to reward your pup the biscuit after he leaves it alone. ~ Enjoy

- Gradually phase out clicking and treating your dog every time that on command he obeys the "leave it" command. Begin gradually reducing treating by only treating one out of two times, one out three times, then one out of four, five, six, and finally none. Do not decrease too quickly. Observe your dog's abilities and pace. The goal is that your dog will obey all the commands without a reward, and only by a vocal or physical cue.

~ Paws On – Paws Off ~

"Down"

Teaching your Beardie to lie down helps to keep your dog in one spot, calms your dog down, and it is a useful action to supersede barking. When paired with stay you can use it to keep your dog comfortably in one place for long periods. This is another very useful command that you will implement throughout the lifetime with your dog.

Basics – "Down!"

- Find that quiet place with low distractions and bring plenty of treats. Wait for your dog to lie down of his own will and then *click and treat* while he is lying down. Toss a treat to get him up again. Keep doing this until he lies down directly after he gets the treat. This means that your dog is starting to understand that good things come to him when he lies down, so in anticipation he is lying right back down.

- Now, continue shaping the action. As soon as your dog starts to lie down, say "down," and *click and treat*. From here on, only *click and treat* your dog when he lies down when you command.

- Next, practice this in other places, for instance in areas with different distractions. Begin practicing indoors, then in the front and back yards; take it on down the block from your house. Be patient in the more distracting locations.

Command your dog to lie down in a variety of situations, such as when strangers are around, when there is food on the table, stereo or television is on, outdoors, barbequing, at a party, in the park, during walking breaks, and so forth. Keep practicing in all situations you encounter and continue gradually increasing the distractions in which you command "down," and your dog complies.

Down is a powerful command, and it will be useful for the life of your dog. Later add "down-stay" to keep your dog in place until you release him or her. It is wonderful when doggie accompanies you to the local morning coffee café, a place where you need your dog to lie quietly beside you whilst you drink your morning coffee, absolutely delightful!

Monitor your dog's progress as you increase the distractions, take note where and when he needs more work relaxing to obey the down command.

- Gradually phase out clicking and treating your dog every time that on command he obeys the "down" command. Begin gradually reducing treating by only treating one out of two times, one out three times, then one out of four, five, six, and finally none. Do not decrease too quickly. Observe your dog's abilities and pace. The goal is that your dog will obey all the commands without a reward, and only by a vocal or physical cue.

PROBLEMS SOLVED

- If he will not lie down, a good location for teaching him is in the bathroom. Unless your dog likes decorative bath soaps, and he may, there is not much to distract him in the bathroom. Because of the tight space, there is usually little else for your dog to do.

- If your dog does lie down but pops right back up, be sure that you are treating him when in the lying down position. This way your dog will be quicker to understand the correlation between the command, action, and treat.

~ Paws On – Paws Off ~

"Stay," Right There Mister

Stay is probably the command that you cannot wait to teach. After all, it is up there as one of the most useful, used, and must know commands. This command can be paired with sit and down, thus making your life easier. Teaching your dog self-control has practical uses such as the good behavior of waiting for you, not running out the door, allowing handling, and not jumping up on people. "Stay" is a highly useful command to teach your dog patience and reinforce that you are in charge of making the decisions about when your dog will do things. This is an easy command to teach after you have taught your dog "sit" and "down" and they make a perfect pairing.

- To begin, find yourselves a quiet low distraction place, and bring plenty of treats. Give the "sit" command, and after he obeys, wait two-seconds before you *click and treat* your dog. Continue practicing while gradually extending the duration to 2, 4, 6, 8 seconds until your dog will sit for duration of ten seconds before receiving a click and treat.

Begin to use the phrase "sit- stay," when issuing this command. At the stay part, add a hand signal. This signal can be your flat hand towards your dog at about a foot or so from his fuzzy little face. You can also use the physical cue of your choosing.

- If your dog gets up, it means you are moving too quickly. Try again with a shorter stay time goal, and then gradually increase the time for your dog to stay. Continue practicing until your dog will stay for 10, 20, or 30, seconds. Keep track of your progress through each training session by starting a training log, so that you know the next duration goal.

- Now, it is time to test your progress.

Say "sit-stay" and take one big step away from your dog, then C/T him for staying. Keep going until you can take two steps in any direction away from your dog without him moving. Make sure that you go back to him to treat each time that he stays. *If he rises or comes to you, do not treat him.*

- Keep doing this until you can take several steps and eventually move out of sight with your dog staying in place. Work until you can get him to stay for two full minutes while you are in his sight, then two or more minutes out of your dog's sight. Continue gradually increasing the time so that your dog will stay no matter what is going on. Many times dogs will lie down after sitting and staying for a number of minutes. Usually after about five minutes, my dog just lies down and stays until I release him.

Now, try all of the above beginning with the "down" command.

- Lastly, begin increasing the distractions, just as we did in teaching the "down" command. Begin practicing indoors, then front and back yards; take it on down the block from your house. Be patient in the more distracting locations. Practice five minutes a day in places with more and more distractions. Continue adding people, animals, and noises to the training sessions. You want your dog to stay during any situation.

- Gradually phase out clicking and treating your dog every time that on command he obeys the "stay" command. Begin gradually reducing treating by only treating one out of two times, one out three times, then one out of four, five, six, and finally none. Do not decrease too quickly. Observe your dog's abilities and pace. The goal is that your dog will obey all the commands without a reward, and only by a vocal or physical cue.

HELPFUL HINTS

- *Always*, reward your dog where he stayed. Do not release him with a "come" command and then treat him. Keep it clear and simple.

- *Change the difficulty*; your dog might decide not to participate if it keeps getting harder and harder all the time. Fluctuate the time that you want your dog to stay.

- Regularly practice the command "stay" before he meets a new person, before he goes out the door (always after you), into the car, and of course during feeding before you put down his food bowl, command "sit stay."

- If you encounter any difficulties, back up a step, and then calmly begin again at a later time. Some dogs take to it quicker than others, so laugh, smile, and roll with it. Enjoy the process while hanging out with your dog.

~ Paws On – Paws Off ~

Going Out On a Leash Here

Training your dog to the leash is probably one of the hardest things you will do. However, in the end, it is very rewarding and can strengthen the trust and bond between you and your dog. There is a variety of collars to choose from, so do some research, and figure out which one is best for your dog. Head collars and front attachment harnesses are a couple of choices. Make sure it fits right, that your dog is comfortable wearing it, and *it is stylish enough so that the other dogs will not mock him.*

Some general rules for choosing a collar are this. If you are small and your dog is large, or your dog tends to be aggressive, you may need the greatest control and choose a head collar. Front attachment collars are a good choice for any dog. Head and frontal attached collars should be used with leashes the length of six feet (1.82 meters) or less. The reason is that a longer length could allow your dog to gain enough speed that he or she could get hurt when they run out of slack and are immediately stopped.

The main goal here is to get your dog to walk beside you *without pulling against the leash.* An easy way to prevent that is to stop moving forward when your dog pulls, and then to reward him with treats when he walks beside you. You can also use praise and affection as a reward. The following steps will help you train your dog to have excellent leash manners. *Loose leash walking is the goal!*

Do not move forward until your dog is regularly performing the expected actions of each step.

Walking With You Is A Treat (The beginning)

Let us begin. Your dog should be wearing a standard harness. Fasten a non-retractable leash that is ten to twenty feet (3-6 meters) long onto the harness. Load up your pouch with top-notch treats and head out to the back yard or a familiar, quiet, low distraction outdoor spot. It is best if there are no other animals or people around.

Decide whether you want your dog to walk on your left or right side, and it is at this side that you choose that you will always treat your dog. Treat your dog at thigh level. Soon, your dog will automatically be coming to that side because that is where the treats can be found. Later you can train your dog to behave the same on the opposite side you choose now. This allows you to walk your dog out of harm's way, and any side of the street no matter where you are walking.

- Begin training. Start walking randomly around the yard. When your dog decides to walk with you, give him a *click and treat* at thigh level of your chosen side. To "walk with you" refers to an appropriate action where you begin to move and your dog walks along with you without pulling in a different direction. If he continues to walk with you on the correct side, give him a *click and treat* with every step or two that you take together. Keep practicing this until your dog is staying by your side more often than not. Do not worry about the treats; you will eventually lessen the frequency then phase them out after he learns this behavior. Deduct the training treats from his next meal.

- Repeat walking around the yard, but this time walk with a faster pace than the first time. When your dog decides to walk with you, give him a *click and treat* at thigh level of your chosen side. Keep practicing this until your dog is staying by your side more often than not. This training will be over multiple sessions and days, so remember to be patient and proceed at your dog's pace. There is no need to rush any training of commands, steps, or sessions.

Eyes on the THIGHS (Second act)

Keeping your dog focused and teaching him that you control the leash actions is crucial. Start walking around the yard again and wait for your dog to lag behind or get distracted by something else. Say, "let's go" to him and slap your thigh to get his attention. Make sure you use a cheerful, welcoming tone. When he pays attention to you, walk away.

- If your dog catches up with you before the leash gets tight, *click and treat* him from your thigh on the chosen side. *Click and treat* him again after he takes a couple of steps with you, and then continue to C/T for the next few steps walking beside you.

- If your dog catches up after the leash gets tight do not treat him, then say, "let's go" again and treat him after he takes a couple of steps with you.

- If he does not come when you say, "let's go" and as the leash gets tight, stop walking and apply some gentle pressure to the leash. When he begins to come toward you praise him. When he gets to you, do not treat him, rather say, "let's go" again. Click and treat your dog if he stays with you, and continue to C/T your dog for every step or two that he stays with you.

- Keep practicing this step until he is staying at your side while you walk around the yard. If he moves away from you say, "let's go" to redirect him, and then C/T him when he returns to walking beside you.

Do not proceed forward until your dog is regularly walking beside you with a loose leash and responding to the "let's go" command. This training can sometimes take many days, just keep practicing until your dog understands and responds to walking beside you while leashed.

Oh the things to smell and pee on (Third act)

Just like you, your dog is going to want to sniff things and go potty. You need to be in control of when your dog does these things. While your dog is on the leash, every five minutes or so, when you would normally treat him, say something like "go sniff," "go play," "free time," or something that you feel comfortable saying, and then, let your dog have some free time on the leash. Keep in mind this is a form of reward, so if he pulls on the leash during this time, say, "let's go," and walk the opposite direction, ending free time quickly and cleanly. If your dog does not pull on the leash when the allotted time has elapsed, you are the one that needs to end the free leash time, so say, "let's go," and walk in the opposite direction.

Where's is my human? (Fourth act)

Continue practicing leash walking in the yard using steps one through three. Gradually, shorten the leash until you have about a 6-foot length. Change direction, change speed, and *click and treat* your dog every time he is able to stay with you during the changes. Now, when he is used to walking by your side you can start phasing out the click and treats, except continue to *click and treat* him when he does something difficult like keeping up with the direction changes, and ignoring other distractions by not pulling on the leash.

Out in the Streets (Fifth act)

Now take your dog out of the back yard and onto the sidewalk for his daily walk. You will use the same techniques you used in your back yard, only now you have to deal with more distractions. Now, you will be dealing with other dogs, animals, friendly strangers, traffic, alarming noises, and who knows what else. This is the time you might consider alternate gear, such as a front attachment harness, or a halter collar, which fits over the head offering ultimate control. Arm yourself with your dog's special treats, be patient, and go slow. Use the "let's go" command when he pulls his leash or forgets that you exist. Give him treats when he walks beside you, and supersize portions if your dog pays attention and does not pull during a stressful moment. Moreover, do not forget *breaks for sniffing and exploring*, those are rewards too.

My friends Boston's love to sniff and pee, but they are curious about everything; those two would make great human naturalists. They constantly have to be reminded that humans are in control of their exploratory missions.

Stop and Go exercise (Sixth act)

Have a 6-foot leash attached to the collar. Hold the leash and toss a treat or toy about twenty feet (6 meters) ahead and start walking toward it. If your dog pulls the leash and tries to get the treat, use the "let's go" command and walk in the opposite direction of the treat. If he stays beside you while you walk toward the treat allow him have it as a reward. Practice this several times until your dog no longer pulls toward the treat but stays at your side and waits for you to walk. Remember that you should be in control of sniffing and potty stops.

Switching Sides (Seventh Act)

After your dog is trained to your chosen side and a few months has passed and both of you are very comfortable with leashed walking, and your dog is walking appropriately, then you can begin training again from the opposite side that you two have trained. There is no rush, proceed training the opposite side when you know it is the right time. Having a dog that can walk obediently leashed on either side is the ultimate goal for navigating the outside world when your dog is leashed.

TROUBLE SHOOTING

- If your dog is crossing in front of you make your presence known to him. He may be distracted.

- If your dog is lagging behind you, he might be frightened or not feeling well. Give him a lot of encouragement instead of pulling him along. If the lagging is due to sniffing or frequent potty breaks, keep walking. In this case, apply only gentle pressure to the leash.

- Remember to deliver numerous rewards when your dog walks beside you, and pay attention to your dog's moods and behaviors so that you keep a good healthy bond between the two of you. Know when your dog is tiring and end the training session on a high note, add playful tones in your voice, and a "good dog" followed by a petting, or some play.

Heel

This is a great command to teach your dog when you encounter distractions, such as other dogs, traffic, construction danger, or just about anything, that warrants keeping your dog close to you so that he does not get into trouble or danger. The heel command is to let your dog know that *until you say otherwise,* he needs to come and remain close beside you while walking.

- Begin this inside or your back yard low distraction area. First, place a treat in your fist on the chosen side of your body. Let him sniff the fist and say "heel" then, take a few steps leading him along with the treat in your fist at thigh level. Click and treat him when he is following your fist with his nose.

- Next, have an *empty fist*, say "heel," and have your dog follow at your side. When he follows your fist for a couple of steps *click and treat* him. Practice this for half dozen or more repetitions.

- Continue to practice heel, but now increase the length of time before you treat him while you are moving around, changing direction or some new serpentine maneuver. This closed empty fist will remain as your physical hand cue for your dog to heel by your side. Use the closed fist at your side when you issue your heel command.

- Now, try this outside of your back yard and in increasingly more distracting situations.

Continue to practice this command each time you take your dog out on the leash. Keeping it fresh will ease your mind because you will know that your dog will comply when necessary. Out in the crazy, nutty, world of ours there are plenty of instances when you will use this command to avoid unnecessary confrontations or circumstances. If you choose to use a different command other than heel pick a word that is uncommon in everyday language, such as "krick," "pickle," or "zing." *~ Paws On – Paws Off ~*

"Go" West Young Beardie

"Go" is a great cue to get your Beardie into his crate or onto his mat or rug, and later his *stuffed goose down micro-fiber plush bed*. This is a very handy command to send your dog to a specific location and keep him there while you tend to your business. Before teaching, "go," your dog should already be performing to the commands, *down*, *stay*, and of course responding to his or her *name*.

While training the following steps, do not proceed to the next step until your dog is regularly performing the current step.

- Find a quiet low distraction location to place a towel or mat on the floor and grab your treats. Put a treat in your hand and use it to lure your dog onto the towel while saying, "go." When all four paws are on the towel, *click and treat* your dog. Do this about ten to fifteen times.

- Start the same way as above, say "go," but this time have an empty hand, act as though you have a treat in your fist while you are luring your dog onto the mat. When all fours are on the mat *click and treat* your dog. Do this ten to fifteen times.

- Keep practicing with an empty hand and eventually turning the empty hand into a pointed index finger. Point your finger towards the mat. If your dog does not understand, walk him to the mat then click and treat. Do this about ten to fifteen times.

- Now, cue with "go" *while pointing* to the towel, but do not walk to the towel with him. If your dog will not go to the towel when you point and say the command, then keep practicing the step above before trying this step again. Now proceed practicing the command "go" while using the pointed finger and when your dog has all four paws on the mat, click, and then walk over and treat him while he is on the mat. Do this about ten to fifteen times.

- Now, grab your towel and try this on different surfaces and other places, such as grass, tile, patio, carpet, and in different rooms. Continue to practice this in more and more distracting situations and don't forget your towel or mat. Take the mat outdoors, to your friends and families houses, hotel rooms, the cabin, and any other place that you have your trusted companion with you.

One Step Beyond – "Relax"

In accordance with "go" This is an extra command you can teach. This is a single command word that encapsulates the command words go, down, and stay all into one word. The purpose is to teach your dog to go to a mat and lie on it until he is released. This is for when you need your dog out from under foot for extended lengths of time, such as when you are throwing a party. Pair it with "down and stay" so your dog will go the mat, lie down, and plan on staying put for an extended period of time. You can substitute your own command, such as "settle," "rest," or "chill," but once you choose a command stick with it and remain consistent.

This command can be used anywhere that you go, letting your dog know that he will be relaxing for a long period and to assume his relaxed posture. You can train this command when your pup is young and it will benefit you and him throughout your life together.

- Place your mat, rug, or what you plan using for your dog to lie upon.

- Give the "go" command and C/T your dog when he has all four paws on the mat. While your dog is on the mat, issue the command "down stay," then go to him and C/T while your dog is still on the mat.

- Now, give the "relax" command and repeat the above exercise with this "relax" command. Say, "relax," "go" and C/T your dog when he has all four paws on the mat. While your dog is on the mat, issue the command "down stay," and C/T while your dog is still on the mat. When your dog understands the "relax" command it will incorporate go, down, and stay.

Practice 7-10 times per session until your dog is easily going to his mat, lying down, and staying in that position until you release him.

- Next, give only the "relax" command and wait for your dog to go to the mat and lie down *before* you *click and treat* your dog. Do not use any other cues at this time. Continue practicing over multiple sessions, 7-10 repetitions per session, so that your dog is easily following your one word instruction of "relax."

- Now begin making it more difficult; vary the distance, add distractions, and increase the times in the relax mode. This is a wonderful command for keeping your dog out of your way for lengthy durations. You will love it when this command is flawlessly followed.

HELPFUL HINT

-While you are increasing the time that your dog maintains his relaxed position, click and treat every 5-10 seconds.

- You can also shape this command so that your dog assumes a more relaxed posture than when you issue "down stay." When your dog realizes that the "relax" command encompasses the super relaxed posture that he would normally use under relaxed conditions, he will understand that he will most likely be staying put for a lengthy period of time and your dog might as well get very comfortable.

Another obedience command that can and should be taught is the release command. Do not forget to teach a release command word to release your dog from any previous command. Release is command #14 in my 49 ½ Dog Tricks book that will soon, or is already for purchase. *Release* is easier to train if your dog already *sits* and *stays* on command. This command informs your dog that they are free to move from whichever previous command you had issued and your dog complied, such as *sit, down,* or *stay.* If you have told your dog to stay, he will sit patiently while you grab his food bowl to fill it, he should remain in the sitting position until released by issuance of the release command. This goes for other things such as when you have issued "sit-stay" and your dog is patiently waiting to enter into your vehicle, and you do not want your dog moving until released. This is an obedience command that can keep your dog safe and you from worrying about your dog bolting off or moving at the wrong time during a potentially dangerous situation. You can choose any command, such as "move," or "now," and so forth. As a reminder, one or two syllable words work best when teaching dogs commands. *~ Paws On – Paws Off ~*

Housetraining the Pup

The fact is, dogs are a bit particular about where they "potty" and will invariably build a very strong habit. When housetraining your puppy, remember that whenever he goes *potty somewhere* in the house, he is building a strong preference to that particular area. This is why preventing potty accidents is very important; additionally thoroughly cleaning the area where the defecation occurred is important. When your puppy does relieve his self in the house, *blame yourself*. Until your puppy has learned where he is supposed to do his business, you should keep a constant, watchful eye on him, whether he is in his crate, on a mat, beside you, or on the couch. While potty training, some people will tether their puppies to their waist. This allows them to keep their puppies in eyesight.

- When your pup is indoors but out of the crate, watch for sniffing or circling, and as soon as you see this behavior, take him outdoors right away. *Do not hesitate.*

- If your pup is having accidents in the crate, the crate may be too big. The crate should be big enough for your puppy to stand up, turn around, and lie down in. If crate accidents occur, remove any soiled items from the crate and thoroughly clean it.

- Set a timer to go off every hour so that you remember to take your puppy out before nature calls. With progress, you can increase the time duration between potty stops.

Some Toy dogs need to go more frequently, around every forty-five minutes.

- If your pup does not do his *duty* when taken outdoors, bring him back indoors and keep a close eye on him. One option is to keep your pup tethered to your waist so that he is always in eyesight, then try again in 10-15 minutes.

Establish a Schedule

- You should take your puppy out many times during the day, most importantly after eating, playing, or sleeping. Feed your puppy appropriate amounts of food two or three times per day and leave the food down for around fifteen-minutes at a time, then remove. You can keep a pups water down until about eight at night, but then remove it from your puppy's reach.

- Puppies can generally hold for a good one-hour stretch. Larger breeds of dogs can hold their bladders longer than smaller dog breeds. Some small dogs cannot last the night before needing to go outside. Most adult dogs generally do not go longer than 8-10 hours between needing to urinate.

- Gradually your puppy will be able to hold urinating for increasingly longer lengths of time, but until then keep to the every hour schedule. Keeping your puppies excrement outdoors, fast tracks your puppy's potty training success.

Consistency Is the Mother of Prevention

Until your puppy is reliably housetrained, bring him outside to the same spot each time, always leaving a little bit of his waste there as a scent marker. This will be the designated potty spot. If you like, place a warning sign at that spot. Remember to use this spot for potty only, and not for play. Bring your puppy to his spot, and when you see him getting ready to go potty, say something like "potty time," "hurry up," or "now." As your pup is going, do not speak because it will distract him. Instead, ponder how much fun it will be when he is playing fetch and running back to you. When your puppy finishes, praise, pet, give a top-notch treat, and spend about five minutes playing with him. If he does not go potty, take your pup inside, keep an eye on him, and try again in 10-15 minutes.

If your puppy goes in the house, remember, that it is *your fault*. Maybe you went too quickly. If you see your puppy relieving himself in the wrong spot, quickly bring him outside to the designated potty spot so that he can finish, then when he is done, offer praise for finishing there. If you find a mess, clean it thoroughly without your puppy watching you do it. Use a cleaner specifically for pet stains so that there is no smell or evidence that you have failed him. This way it will not become a regular spot for your puppy and a new regular clean up chore for you.

This Question Rings a Bell: Can I teach my puppy when to tell me when he needs to go out?

- Yes, you can! Hang a bell at dog level beside the door you use to let your dog outdoors. Put some easy cheese or peanut butter on the bell. When he touches it and rings it, immediately open the door. Repeat this every time and take him to the potty spot. Eventually, he will ring the bell without the easy cheese and this will tell you when he needs to go outside. Be careful here, your puppy may start to ring the bell when he wants to go outside to play, explore, or other non-potty reasons. To avoid this, each time he rings the bell, *only* take him out to the potty spot. If he starts to play, immediately bring him in the house.

Small Dogs often take longer time to potty train. I really do not know why, they just do. One way to help is to take them out more often than you would a larger dog. The longest duration I would go without taking a small dog to the potty spot is about 4 hours, and as a puppy maybe forty-five minutes instead of an hour. In addition, many small or toy dogs do well with a litter box. This way, they can go whenever nature calls and whatever the situation is, such as when there is an ice storm outside and they refuse to get their tiny little paws cold. Because many are easily chilled, some small dogs tend to dislike going outside during foul weather, or even cool conditions. Concurrently, we do not enjoy it either.

~ Paws On – Paws Off ~

Chewing

All puppies love and enjoy chewing, especially while teething, but a chewing Beardie can do some serious damage, so be alert and diligent to thwart that behavior so it does not get out of hand. Keep many toys and doggy chews around so that you can redirect your puppy towards the dog specific toys, and not your new black leather shoes.

Let your pup know that his or her toys are the only acceptable items to be chewed. Loneliness, boredom, fear, teething, and separation anxiety, are feelings that can motivate your puppy into chewing. Until you have trained that *chewing only happens with dog toys*, you can leave your pup in his crate while you are away. Be sure to throw some dog chewy toys in the crate.

Lots of physical exercise, training, and mental challenges will assist in steering your dog away from destructive chewing. Until your puppy is over his "I'll chew anything phase," hide your shoes and other items that you do not want chewed, thus temporarily puppy proofing your home. The "leave it!" command should be trained so you can quickly steer your pup away from anything that is not his to chew. Avoid letting your dog mouth or chew on your fingers or hand, because that can lead to biting behaviors.

~ Paws On – Paws Off ~

Jumping Jeepers

Your dog loves you and wants as much attention from you as possible. The reality is that you are the world to your dog. Often when your dog is sitting quietly, he is easily forgotten. When he is walking beside you, you are probably thinking about other things, such as work, dinner, the car, chores you need to accomplish, or anything but your loyal companion walking next to you. Sometimes your dog receives your full attention only when he jumps up on you. When your dog jumps up on you, then you look at him, physically react in astonishment, maybe shout at him, and gently push him down until he is down on the floor. Then, you ignore him again, and make a mental note to teach your dog not to jump up onto you. What do you expect? He wants your attention. Teaching your dog not to jump is essentially teaching him that attention will come only if he has all four paws planted firmly on the ground.

It is important not to punish your dog when teaching him not to jump up on you and others. Do not shout "no!" or "bad!" Do not knee your dog or push him down. The best way to handle the jumping is to turn your back and ignore your dog. Remember, since he loves you very much, your dog or puppy may take any physical contact from you as a positive sign. You do not want to send mixed signals; instead, you want to practice complete ignoring that consists of no looking or audio. If you do use a vocal command, do not say, "off," instead use "sit," which your dog has probably already learned. Try not to use a command, and instead proceed with ignoring.

For jumping practice, it would be ideal if you could gather a group of people together who will participate in helping you train your dog that jumping is a no-no. You want to train your dog to understand that he will only get attention if he is on the ground. If groups of people are not available, then teach him to remain grounded using his family. When your dog encounters other people, use a strong "sit stay" command to keep all four paws planted firmly on the ground. I covered "sit stay" above, and now you understand how useful and versatile this command can be.

No Jumping On the Family

This is the easiest part, because the family and frequent visitors have more chances to help your dog or puppy to learn. When you come in from outside and your dog starts jumping up, say, "oops!" or "whoa," and immediately leave through the same door. Wait a few seconds after leaving and then do it again. When your dog finally stops jumping upon you as you enter, give him a lot of attention. Ask the rest of the family to follow the same protocol when they come into the house. If you find that he is jumping up at other times as well, like when you sing karaoke, walking down the hallway, or are cooking at the barbeque, just ignore your dog by turning your back and put energy into giving him attention when he is sitting.

No Jumping on Others

Prevention is of utmost importance and the primary focus in this exercise, especially with larger dogs. You can prevent your dog from jumping by using a leash, a tieback, crate, or gate. Until you have had enough practice and your dog knows what you want him to do, you really should use one of these methods to prevent your dog from hurting someone or getting an inadvertent petting reward for jumping. To train, you will need to go out and solicit some dog training volunteers and infrequent visitors to help.

- Make what is called a *tieback*, which is a leash attached to something sturdy, within sight of the doorway but not blocking the entrance keeping your dog a couple of feet or about a meter away from the doorway. Keep this there for a few months during the training period until your dog is not accosting you or visitors. When the guest arrives, hook your dog to the secure leash and then let the guest in.

Guests Who Want to Help Train Your Dog (Thank you in advance)

All of these training sessions may take many sessions to complete, so remain patient and diligent in training and prevention until your dog complies with not jumping on people.

- Begin at home, and when a guest comes in through the door, and the dog jumps up, they are to say "oops" or "whoa," and leave immediately. Practice this with at least five or six different visitors, each making multiple entrances during the same visit. If your helpers are jumped, have them completely ignore your dog by not making any eye contact, physical or vocal actions other than the initial vocal word towards your dog, then have them turn their backs and immediately leave.

- When you go out onto the streets, have your dog leashed. Next, have your guest helper approach your dog. If he strains against the leash or jumps have the guest turn their back and walk away. When your dog calms himself and sits, have the guest approach again. Repeat this until the guest can approach, pet and give attention to your dog without your dog jumping up. Have the volunteer repeat this at least five to seven times. Remember to go slowly and let your dog have breaks. Keep the sessions in the 5-7 minute range. For some dogs, this type of training can get frustrating. Eventually, your dog will understand that his jumping equals being ignored.

- Use the tie-back that you have placed near the door. Once your dog is calm, the visitor can greet your dog if they wish. If the guest does not wish to greet your dog, give your dog a treat to calm his behavior. If he barks, send your dog to his crate or the gated time out area. The goal is that you always greet your guests first, *not your dog*. Afterward, your guests have the option to greet or not greet, instead of your dog always rushing in to greet every guest. If he is able to greet guests calmly while tied back, then he may be released. At first hold the leash to see how your dog reacts, then if he is calm release him.

A Caveat to These Two Methods

1) For those who are not volunteers to help teach your dog and are at your home visiting, there is another method. Keep treats by the door, and as you walk in throw them seven to nine feet (2.1 - 2.7 meters) away from you. Continue doing this until your dog begins to anticipate this. Once your dog is anticipating treats every time someone comes through the door it will keep him from accosting you or visitors that walk through the doorway. After your dog eats his treat and he has calmed down a bit, ask him to sit, and then give him some good attention.

2) Teach your dog that a hand signal such as grabbing your left shoulder means the same as the command "sit." By

combining the word "sit" with a hand on your left shoulder, he will learn this. If you want to use another physical cue, you can substitute your own gesture here, such as holding your left wrist or ear.

Ask the guests that have volunteered to help train your dog to place their right hand on their left shoulders and wait until your dog *sits* before they pet him or give any attention. Training people that meet your dog will help both you and your dog in preventing unwanted excitement and jumping up. Having your dog sit before he can let loose with jumps is proactive jumping prevention.

~ Paws On – Paws Off ~

Barking Madness

Any dog owner knows that dogs bark for many reasons, most commonly, for attention. Your Beardie may bark for play, attention, or because it is close to feeding time and he wants you to feed him. Dogs also bark to warn intruders and us so we also need to understand why our dog is barking. Not all barking is bad. Some dogs are short duration barkers, and others can go on for hours, we do not want that and either do our neighbors.

Whatever the case, *don't do it*. Do not give your dog attention for barking. Do not send the signals that your dogs barking gets an immediate reaction from you, such as you coming to see why he is barking or moving towards him. As I mentioned in the opening paragraph, they do sometimes bark to warn us, so we shouldn't ignore all barking, we need to assess the barking situation before dismissing it as nonsense barking. When you know the cause is a negative behavior that needs correction, say, "leave it" and ignore him. While not looking at your dog go to the other side of the room, or into another room, you can even close the door behind you until your dog has calmed down. Make it clear to your barking dog that his barking does not result in any rewards or attention.

In everyday life, make sure you are initiating activities that your dog enjoys and always making them happen on *your* schedule. You are the alpha leader so regularly show your pup who is in charge. Also, make sure that he earns what he is provided. Have your pup *sit* before he gets the reward of going outside to play, a toy, his bowl of food, or loaded into the car to go tailgating (home team jersey not included).

Your dog may bark when seeing or hearing something interesting. Below are a few ways to deal with this issue.

Prevention when you are at your residence

- *Teach your dog the command "quiet."* When your dog barks, wave a piece of food in front of his nose at the same time you are saying, "quiet." When he stops barking to sniff, *click and treat* him right away. Do this about four or five times. Then the next time he barks, pretend you have a piece of food in your hand next to his nose and say, "quiet." Always *click and treat* him as soon as he *stops* barking. After issuing the "quiet" command, *click and treat* him again for every few seconds that he remains quiet. Eventually, as you make your way to five or ten seconds, gradually increase the time lapses between the command "quiet," and *clicking and treating*.

- *Prevent it.* Block the source of sound or sight so that your dog is unable to see or hear the catalyst that is sparking his barking. Use a fan, stereo, T.V., curtains, blinds, or simply put him in a different area of the house to keep him away from the stimulus.

- When your pup hears or sees something that would usually make him bark and he *does not bark*, reward him with attention, play, or a treat. This is reinforcing and shaping good behaviors instead of negative behaviors.

The Time Out

- We use it on our children, and yes you can you can use a *time out* on your dog, but do not use it too often. When you give your dog a time out, you are taking your dog out of his social circle and giving your dog what is known as a negative punishment. This kind of punishment is powerful and can have side effects that you do not want. Your dog may begin to fear you when you walk towards him, especially if you have the irritated look on your face that he recognizes as the *time out face*. The *time out* should be used very sparingly. Focus on teaching your dog the behaviors that you prefer while preventing the bad behavior.

Choose a place where you want the time out spot to be. Make sure that this place is not the potty spot, the play area, or the *Saturday night square dancing spot*. Ideally it is a boring place that is somewhere that is not scary, not too comfortable, but safe. A gated pantry or the bathroom can work well. If your puppy does not mind his crate, you can use it. Secure a 2-foot piece of rope or a short leash to your puppy's collar. When your pup barks, use a calm voice and give the command, "time out," then take the rope and walk him firmly but gently to the time out spot. Leave him there for about 5 minutes, longer if necessary. When your dog is calm and not barking you can release him. You may need to do this two to a dozen times before he understands which behavior has put him into the time out place. Most dogs are social and love being around their humans, so this can have a strong impact.

Prevention when you are away from your residence

- Again, prevent barking by blocking the sounds or sights that are responsible for your dog or puppy going into barking mode. Use a fan, stereo, curtain, blinds, or keep him in another part of the house away from the stimulus.

- Use a Citronella Spray Collar. Only use this for when the barking has become intolerable. Do not use this when the barking is associated with fear or aggression. You will want to use this a few times when you are at home, so that your dog understands how it works.

Citronella collars work like this. The collar has a sensitive microphone, which senses when your dog is barking, when this happens it triggers a small release of citronella spray into the area above a dog's nose. It surprises the dog and disrupts barking by emitting a smell that dogs dislike.

Out walking

While you are out walking your dog, out of shear excitement or from being startled, he might bark at other dogs, people, cars, and critters. This can be a natural reaction or your dog may have sensitivities to certain tones, the goal is to try to limit the behavior and quickly cease the barking.

Here are some helpful tools to defuse that behavior.

- Teach your dog the *"watch me"* command. Begin this training in the house where there are fewer distractions. While you hold a treat to your nose, say your dog's name and "watch me." When your dog looks at the treat for at least one second give him a click and treat. Repeat this about 10-15 times. Then increase the time that your dog looks at you to 2-3 seconds, and repeat a dozen times.

- Then, repeat the process while pretending to have a treat on your nose. You will then want to incorporate this hand to your nose as your hand signal for *watch me. Click and treat* when your dog looks at you for at least one second, then increase to two or three seconds, and *click and treat* after each goal. Repeat this about 10-15 times.

- Increase the duration that your dog will continue to watch you while under the command. Continue practicing while increasing the length of time your dog will watch you. Click and treat as your progress. Try to keep your dogs attention for 5-10 seconds. Holding your dog's attention for this length of time usually results in the catalyst to move away from the area or for your dog to lose interest.

- Now, practice the "watch me" command while you are walking around inside the house. Then practice this again outside. When outside, practice near something he finds interesting. Practice in a situation that he would normally bark. Continue practicing in different situations and around other catalysts that you know will set your dog off barking.

This is a great way to steer attention towards you and away from your dog's barking catalysts.

Other Solutions

- When you notice something that normally makes your dog bark and he has not begun to bark, use the "quiet" command. For example, your dog regularly barks at the local skateboarder. When the trigger that provokes your dog's barking, the skateboarder comes zooming by, use the command "quiet," and *click and treat*. Click and treat your dog for every few seconds that he remains quiet. Teach your dog that his barking trigger gets him a "quiet" command. Your dog will begin to associate the skateboarder with treats and gradually it will diminish his barking outbursts at the skateboarder.

- If he frequently barks while a car is passing by, put a treat by his nose, and then bring it to your nose. When he looks at you, *click and treat* him. Repeat this until he voluntarily looks at you when a car goes by and does not bark, continuing to *treat* him appropriately.

 - You can also reward your dog for calm behavior. When you see something or encounter something that he would normally bark at and he does not, *click and treat* your dog. Instead of treats, sometimes offer praise and affection

- If you are out walking and your dog has not yet learned the *quiet* cue, or is not responding to it, turn around and walk away from whatever is causing your dog to bark. When he calms down, offer a reward.

- As a last resort use the citronella spray collar if your dogs barking cannot be controlled using the techniques that you have learned. Use this only when the barking is *not* associated with fear or aggression.

Your dog is Afraid, Aggressive, Lonely, Territorial, or Hung-over

Your dog may have outbursts when he feels territorial, aggressive, lonely, or afraid. All of these negative behaviors can be helped with proper and early socialization, but occasionally they surface. Many times rescue dogs might have not been properly socialized and bring their negative behaviors into your home. Be patient while you are teaching your new dog proper etiquette. Some breeds, especially watch and guarding breeds are prone to territorialism and it can be a challenge to limit their barking.

- This is not a permanent solution, but is a helpful solution while you are teaching your dog proper barking etiquette.

To allow your dog a chance to find his center, relax his mind and body, do this for about seven to ten days before beginning to train against barking. As a temporary solution, you should first try to prevent outbursts by crating, gating, blocking windows, using fans or music to hide sounds, and avoid taking your dog places that can cause these barking outbursts.

SOME TIPS

- Always, remain calm, because a relaxed and composed alpha achieves great training outcomes. A confident, calm, cool, and collected attitude that states you are unquestionably in charge goes a long way in training.

- If training is too stressful or not going well, you may want to hire a professional positive trainer for private sessions. When interviewing, tell him or her that you are using a clicker and rewards based training system and are looking for a trainer that uses the same type or similar methods.

It is important to help your dog to modify his thinking about what tends to upset him. Teach him that what he was upset about before now predicts his favorite things. Here is how.

- When the trigger appears in the distance, *click and treat* your dog. Keep clicking and treating your dog as the two of you proceed closer to the negative stimulus.

- If he is territorially aggressive, teach him that the doorbell or a knock on the door means that is his cue to get into his crate and wait for treats. You can do this by ringing the doorbell and uring your dog to his crate and once he is inside the crate giving him treats.

- You can also lure your dog through his fears. If you are out walking and encounter one of his triggers, put a treat to his nose and lead him out and away from the trigger zone.

- Use the "watch me" command when you see him getting nervous or afraid. *Click and treat* him frequently for watching you.

- Reward *calm* behavior with praise, toys, play, or treats.

- *For the hangover, I recommend lots of sleep.*

Your dog is frustrated, bored or both

All dogs including your dog or puppy may become bored or frustrated. At these times, your dog may lose focus, not pay attention to you, and *spend time writing bad poetry in his journal*. Here are a few things that can help prevent this:

- Keep him busy and tire him out with chew toys, exercise, play, and training. These things are a cure for most negative behaviors. A tired dog is usually happy to relax and enjoy quiet time.

- He should have at least 30 minutes of aerobic exercise per day. In addition to the aerobic exercise, each day he should have an hour of chewing and about 15 minutes of training. Keep it interesting for him with a variety of activities. It is, after all, the spice of life.

- Use the command "quiet" or give your dog a time out.

- As a last resort, you can break out the citronella spray collar.

Excited to Play

- Like an actor in the wings, your puppy will get excited about play. Teach your dog that when he starts to bark, the play stops. Put a short leash on him and if he barks, use it to lead him out of play sessions. Put your dog in a time out or just stop playing with your dog. Reward him with more play when he calms down.

Armed with these many training tactics to curb and stop barking, you should be able to gradually reduce your dogs barking, and help him to understand that some things are not worth barking at all. Gradually you will be able to limit the clicking and treating, but it is always good practice to reward your dog for not barking and behaving in the manner you desire. Reward your dog with supersized treat servings for making the big breakthroughs.

~ Paws On – Paws Off ~

The Ole Nipperdoggie

Friendly puppies nip for a few reasons; they are teething, playing or they want to get your attention. My Uncle Jimmy nips from a bottle, but that is a completely different story. Not to worry, in time most puppies will naturally grow out of this behavior. Other herding dogs nip as a herding instinct that comes from their heritage. They do this to round up their animal charges, other animals, and or family members.

While your dog is working through the nipping stage, you will want to avoid punishing or correcting your dog because this could eventually result in a strained relationship down the road. You also want to teach your puppy how delicate human skin is. Let your dog test it out and give him feedback. Say, "yipe,", 'youch!" or "Bowie," and pull your hand back when he nips too hard. Furthermore, cease offering any further attention towards your dog. If you act more and more sensitive to the nips, he will understand the fact that humans are very sensitive and will respond accordingly.

This is a very easy behavior to modify because we know the motivation behind it. The puppy wants to play and chew and who doesn't? Give your dog access to a variety of chew toys, and when he nips, walk away and ignore him. If he follows you, and nips at your heels, give your dog a time out. Afterward, when your dog is relaxed and gentle, stay and play with him. Use the utmost in patience with your puppy. In time this will pass.

Herding dogs will not so easily be dissuaded, and it is not always possible to curb this behavior entirely, but you can try to limit or soften it, possibly getting through to them that nipping humans is a No-No and painful.

Preventing the Nippage

- Have a chew toy in your hand when you are playing with your puppy. This way he learns what the right thing is to bite and chew, and it is not your heels or hand.

- Get rid of your puppy's excess energy by exercising him *at least* an hour each day. As a result, he will have no energy to nip.

- Make sure he is getting enough rest and he is not cranky. Twelve hours per day is good for dogs, and it seems for teenagers as well.

- Always, have lots of interesting chew toys available to help your puppy through the teething process.

- Teach your kids not to run away screaming from nipping puppies. They should walk away quietly or simply stay still. Children should not be left unsupervised when around dogs and puppies.

- As a last resort, when the other items discussed above are not working, you increase the frequency of using a tieback to hold your dog, a`nd gated or time out areas.

Instructing Around the Nippage

- Play with your dog and praise him for being gentle. When he nips say, *"yipe!"* like a puppy would say and immediately walk away. After the nipping, wait one minute and then return to give him another chance to play or just be in your presence without nipping. Practice this for two or three minutes and remember to give everyone who will have daily contact with the puppy a chance to play and train him.

- Use a tieback to secure your pup, or put him in a room with a small gate that you can easily climb over. Always use a tieback while your dog is under supervision.

The tieback is a useful method and can be utilized for other attention getting behaviors like jumping, barking, and the dreaded leg humping.

~ Paws On – Paws Off ~

Some Digging Help

Some dogs are going to dig no matter what you do to stop it. For these diggers, this behavior is bred into them, so remember that these dogs have an urge to do what they do. Whether this behavioral trait is for hunting or foraging, it is deeply imbedded inside their DNA and it is something that cannot be turned off easily, or at all. Remember that when you have a digger for a dog, they will tend to be excellent escape artists, so you will need to bury your perimeter fencing deep to keep them inside your yard or kennel.

Cold weather dogs such as Huskies, Malamutes, Chows, and other "Spitz" type dogs often dig a shallow hole in an area to lie down in, to either cool down, or warm up. These dogs usually dig in a selected and distinct area, such as in the shade of a tree or shrub.

Other natural diggers such as Terriers, and Dachshunds, are natural hunters and dig to bolt or hold prey at bay for their hunting companions. These breeds have been genetically bred for the specific purpose of digging into holes to chase rabbits, hare, badgers, weasels, and other burrowing animals. Scenthounds such as Beagles, Bassets, and Bloodhounds will dig under fences in pursuit of their quarry. This trait is not easily altered or trained away, but you can steer it into the direction of your choosing. To combat dog escapes you will need to bury your fencing or chicken wire deep into the ground. It is suggested that 18-24 inches, or 46-61cm into the soil below the bottom edge of your fencing is sufficient, but we all know that a determined dog may even go deeper, when in pursuit of quarry. Some dog owners will affix chicken wire at about 12 inches (30.5cm) up onto the fence, and then bury the rest down deep into the soil. Usually, when the digging dog reaches the wire, its efforts will be thwarted and it will stop digging.

Some dogs dig as an instinctive impulse to forage for food to supplement their diet. Because dogs are omnivorous, they will sometimes root out tubers, rhizomes, bulbs, or any other edible root vegetable that is buried in the soil. Even nuts buried by squirrels, newly sprouting grasses, the occasional rotting carcass or other attractive scents will be an irresistible aroma to their highly sensitive noses.

Other reasons dogs dig can be traced directly to boredom, lack of exercise, lack of mental and physical stimulation, or improperly or under-socialized dogs. Improperly socialized dogs can suffer from separation anxiety and other behavioral issues. Non-neutered dogs may dig an escape to chase a female in heat. Working breeds such as Border Collies, Australian Cattle Dogs, Shelties, and other working breeds can stir up all sorts of trouble if not kept busy. This trouble can include incessant digging.

It has been said that the smell of certain types of soil can also catch a dog's fancy. Fresh earth, moist earth, certain mulches, topsoil, and even sand are all lures for the digger. If you have a digger, you should fence off the areas where you are using these alluring types of soils. These kinds of soils are often used in newly potted plants or when establishing a flowerbed or garden. The smell of dirt can sometimes attract a dog that does not have the strong digging gene, but when he finds out how joyful digging can be, beware; you can be responsible for the creation of your own "Frankendigger."

Proper socialization, along with plenty of mental and physical exercises will help you in your fight against digging, but as we know, some diggers are going to dig no matter what the situation. Just in case your dog or puppy is an earnest excavator, here are some options to help you curb that urge.

The Digging Pit

A simple and fun solution is to dig a pit specifically for him or her to dig to their little heart's content. Select an appropriate location, and with a spade, turn over the soil a bit to loosen it up, mix in some sand to keep it loose as well as to improve drainage, then surround it with stones or bricks to make it obvious by sight that this is the designated spot.

To begin training your dog to dig inside the pit, you have to make it attractive and worth their while. First bury bones, chews, or a favorite toy, then coax your dog on over to the pit to dig up some treasures. Keep a watchful eye each time you bring your dog out, and do not leave him or her unsupervised during this training time. It is important to halt immediately any digging outside of the pit. When they dig inside of the designated pit, be sure to reward them with treats and praise. If they dig elsewhere, direct them back to the pit. Be sure to keep it full of the soil-sand mixture, and if necessary, littered with their favorite doggie bootie. If your dog is not taking to the pit idea, an option is to make the other areas where they are digging temporarily less desirable such as covering them with chicken wire, and then making the pit look highly tantalizingly, like a *doggie digging paradise*.

Buried Surprises

Two other options are leaving undesirable surprises in the unwanted holes your dog has begun to dig. A great deterrent is to place your dog's own *doodie* into the holes that he has dug, and when your dog returns to complete his job, he will not enjoy the gift you have left him, thus deterring him from further digging.

Another excellent deterrent is to place an air-filled balloon inside the hole and then cover it with soil. When your dog returns to his undertaking and then his little paws burst the balloon, the resulting loud "POP!" sound will startle, and as a result, your dog will reconsider the importance of his or her mission. After a few of these shocking noises, you should have a dog that thinks twice before digging up your bed of pansies.

Shake Can Method

This method requires a soda can or another container filled with rocks, bolts, or coins, remembering to place tape or apply the cap over the open end to keep the objects inside. Keep this "rattle" device nearby so that when you let your dog out into the yard you can take it with you to your clandestine hiding spot. While hidden out of sight, simply wait until our dog begins to dig. Immediately at the time of digging, take that can of coins and shake it vigorously, thereby startling your dog. Repeat the action each time your dog begins to dig, and after a few times your dog should refrain from further soil removal. Remember, the goal is to *startle* and to distract your dog at the time they initiate their digging, and not to terrorize your little friend.

Shake can instructions

1. Shake it quickly once or twice then stop. The idea is to make a sudden and disconcerting noise that is unexpected by your dog who is in the process of digging. If you continue shaking the can, it will become an ineffective technique.

2. Beware not to overuse this method. Remember your dog *can become desensitized* to the sound, and thus ignore the prompt.

3. Sometimes, it is important to supplement this method by using commands, such as "No" or "Stop."

4. Focus these techniques, targeting only the behavior (e.g. digging) that you are trying to eliminate.

5. Sometimes, a noise made by a can with coins inside may not work, but perhaps using a different container filled with nuts and bolts, or other items will. Examples are soda or coffee cans that are filled with coins, nuts, bolts, or other metal objects. You might have to experiment to get an effective and disruptive sound. If the noise you make sets off prolonged barking instead of a quick startled bark, then the sound is obviously not appropriate. If your dog does begin to bark after you make the noise, use the "quiet" command immediately after, and never forget to reward your dog when he or she stops the barking, thereby reinforcing the wanted behavior.

I hope that these methods will assist you in controlling or guiding your four-legged landscaper in your desired direction. Anyone that has had a digger for a dog knows it can be challenging. Just remember that tiring them out with exercise and games is often the easiest and most effective in curbing unwanted behaviors.

~ Paps

~ Paws On – Paws Off ~

PART III
Body Language and Vocals

Training your dog seems like a daunting task, but it is a unique and rewarding experience. It is the foundation of a healthy and long relationship with your new dog or puppy. You must be the one in charge of the relationship and lead with the pack leader mentality, all the while showing patience and love. Whether you choose to enroll your dog in an obedience school such as the Sirius™ reward training system or go it alone at home, you will the need assistance of quality books, videos, and articles to help guide you through the process and find solutions to obstacles along the way.

Without a doubt, it is nice to have an obedient friend by your side through good times and bad. Owning a dog is a relationship that needs tending throughout the years. Once you begin training, it will continue throughout the life of your dog and friend. An obedient dog is easier to care for and causes less household problems and expense. You know what needs to be done, but what about your dog. How do you read his messages in regards to what you are attempting to accomplish? I am going to cover dog's body language and vocal language to provide insight into what it is your dog is trying to tell you. This should prove to be an asset while training your dog.

Body Language:

What is body language? Body language is all of the non-verbal communication we exhibit when engaged into an exchange with another entity. Say what? All of those little tics, spasms, and movements that we act out comprise of non-verbal body language. Studies state that over 50% of how people judge us is based on our use of body language.

Apparently, the visual interpretation of our message is equal to our verbal message. It is interesting how some studies have indicated that when the body language disagrees with the verbal, our verbal message accounts for as little as 7-10% of how the others judge us. With that kind of statistic, I would say that body language is extremely important.

Similar to humans, dogs use their bodies to communicate. Their hearing and seeing senses are especially acute. Observe how your dog tilts his head, moves his legs, and what is his tail doing while you are engaged. Is the tail up, down, or wagging? These body movements are all part of the message your dog is trying to convey. With this knowledge, I think it is safe to say that we should learn a little about human and dog body language. In this article, I will stick to a dog's body language and leave the human investigation up to you. What do you think my posture is right now?

The Tail:

The tail is a wagging and this means the dog is friendly, or maybe not. With most dogs that have tails it can convey many messages, some nice, some nasty. Specialists say a dogs wagging tail can mean the dog is scared, confused, preparing to fight, confident, concentrating, interested, or happy.

How do you tell the difference? Look at the speed and range of motion in the tail. The wide-fast tail wag is usually the message of "Hey, I am so happy to see you!" wag. The tail that is not tight between the hind legs, but instead is sticking straight back horizontally means the dog is curious but unsure, and probably not going to bite but remain in a place of neutral affection. This dog will probably not be confrontational, yet the verdict is not in. The slow tail wag means the same; the dog's friendly meter is gauging the other as friend or foe.

The tail held high and stiff, or bristling (hair raised) is a WATCH OUT! Red Flag warning for humans to be cautious. This dog may not only be aggressive, but dangerous and ready to rumble. If you come across this dog, it is time to calculate your retreat and escape plan.

Not only should the speed and range of the wag be recognized while you are reading doggie body language, one must also take note of the tail position. A dog that is carrying its tail erect is a self-assured dog in control of itself. On the flip side of that, the dog with their tail between their legs, tucked in tight is the, "I surrender man, I surrender, please don't hurt me" posture.

The chill dog, a la Reggae special is the dog that has her tail lowered but not tucked in-between her legs. The tail that is down and relaxed in a neutral position states, the dog is relaxed.

While training your dog or simply playing, it is a good idea to take note of what his or her tail is doing and determine if your dog's tail posture is matching their moods. Your understanding of your dog's tail movements and body posture will be of great assistance throughout its lifetime.

Up Front:

On the front end of the dog is the head and ears with their special motions. A dog that cocks his head or twitches her ears is giving the signal of interest and awareness, but sometimes it can indicate fear. The forward or ear up movements can show a dog's awareness of seeing or hearing something new. Due to the amazingly acute canine sense of hearing, this can occur long before we are aware. These senses are two of the assets that make dogs so special and that make them fantastic guard and watchdogs.

"I give in, and will take my punishment" is conveyed with the head down and ears back. Take note of this submissive posture, observe the neck, and back fur for bristling. Sometimes this accompanies this posture. Even though a dog is giving off this submissive stance, it should be approached with caution because it may feel threatened and launch an offensive attack thinking he needs to defend himself.

"Smile, you are on camera." Yep, you got it, dogs smile too. It is usually a subtle corner pull back to show the teeth. Do not confuse this with the obvious snarl that entails a raised upper lip and bared teeth, sometimes accompanied by a deep growling sound. The snarl is something to be extremely cautious of when encountered. A snarling dog is not joking around--*the snarl is serious*. This dog is ready to be physically aggressive.

The Whole Kit and Caboodle:

Using the entire body, a dog that rolls over onto its back and exposes his belly, neck, and genitals is conveying the message that you are in charge. A dog that is overly submissive sometimes urinates a small amount to express his obedience towards a human or another dog.

Front paws down, rear end up, tail is a waggin.' This, "hut, hut, hut, C'mon Sparky hike the ball," posture is the ole K-9 position of choice for, "Hey! It is playtime, and I am ready to go!" This posture is sometimes accompanied with a playful bark and or pawing of the ground in an attempt to draw you into his playful state. I love it when a dog is in this mood, albeit they can be aloof to commands.

Whines, Growls, Howls, Barks and Yelps. Sounds dogs make and we hear

We just had a look at the silent communication of body language. Now, I will look into the doggie noises we cherish, but sometimes find annoying. Just what is our dog trying to tell us? Our canine friends often use vocal expressions to get their needs met. Whines and growls mean what they say, so when training your dog, listen carefully. As you become accustomed to the dogs vocal communication, and are able to begin understanding them, the happier you will both become. Some dog noises can be annoying and keep you awake, or wake you up. This may need your attention, to be trained out as inappropriate vocalizations.

Barking:

What does a dog bark say and why bark at all? Dogs bark to say "Hey, what's up dude," "I am hungry," or "Look at me!" A bark may warn about trouble, or to convey that the dog is bored or lonely. I think we all know that stimulated and excited dogs also bark. It is up to us to survey the surroundings and assess the reason. We need to educate ourselves about our dog's various barks so we can act appropriately.

Whining and Whimpering:

Almost from the time they are freshly made and feeding upon their mother's milk, our little puppies begin to make their first little fur-ball noises. Whimpering or whining to get their mothers attention for feeding or comfort is innate, and as a result, they know mom will come to them. They also use these two W's on us to gain our attention. Other reasons for whimpering or whining are from fear produced by loud noises such as thunderstorms or fireworks. I think most of us have experienced the 4th of July phenomenon where the entire dog population is barking excessively until the wee hours of the morning when the last fireworks are ignited, and the final "BOOM!" dies off.

Growl:

Growling means, you had better watch out. Be acutely aware of what this dog is doing or might do. Usually a dog that is growling is seriously irritated and preparing to be further aggressive.

Howl:

Picture the dark silhouette of a howling dog with a full moon backdrop. A dog's howl is a distinct vocalization that most dogs use, and every wolf makes. Howling can mean loneliness, desire, warning, or excitement. A lonely howl is a dog looking for a response. Dogs also howl after a long hunt when they have tracked and cornered their prey. Some Scenthounds use a distinct sound named a bay.

~ Paws On – Paws Off ~

Handle Me Gently

Teaching your Beardie to be still, calm, and patient while he is being handled is a very important step in your relationship. When you master this one, it will make life easier for both of you when at home, and either at the groomer or the vet. It also helps when there is unwanted or accidental touching and especially when dealing with small children who love to handle dogs in all sorts of unusual and not so regular ways. This one will take patience and a few tricks to get it started. Remember, it is important to begin handling your new puppy immediately after you find each other and are living together.

Understand that muzzles are not bad and do not hurt dogs. They can be an effective device and a great safety feature when your dog is learning to be handled. Easy cheese or peanut butter spread on the floor or on the refrigerator door should keep your puppy in place while he learns to be handled. If your puppy does not like to be handled, he can slowly learn to accept it.

You must practice this with your puppy for at least one to three minutes each day so that he becomes comfortable with being touched. All dogs are unique and therefore some will accept this easier and quicker than others will. Handling training will be a life-long process.

With all of the following exercises, follow these steps:

- Begin with short, non-intrusive gentle touching. *If your puppy is calm* and he is not trying to squirm away, use a word such as "good," "nice," or "yes," and give your pup a treat.

- If your puppy squirms, keep touching him but do not fight his movements, keeping your hands lightly on him while moving your hand with his squirms. When he settles, treat him and remove your hands.

- Work from one second to ten seconds where applicable, gradually working your way up to touching for longer durations, such as 2,4,6,8 to 10 seconds.

- Do not go forward to another step until your puppy adapts to, and enjoys the current step.

- *Do not* work these exercises more than a couple of minutes at a time. Overstimulation can cause your puppy stress. Continue slowly at your puppy's comfortable speed.

Handling the Body

Paws in the clause

It is a fact that most puppies do not like to have their paws touched. Proceed slowly with this exercise. The eventual goal is for your puppy to adore his paws being fondled. In the following exercises, any time your puppy does not squirm and try to get away, *click and treat* your pup. If he does squirm, stay with him using gentle contact, when your pup ceases wiggling, then *click and treat*, and release when he calms down. Each one of these steps will take a few days to complete and will require at least a dozen repetitions. Make sure you successfully complete each step and your puppy is at least tolerant of the contact before you go on to the next one.

- *Do each step with all four paws, and remember to pause a minute between paws, allowing your pup to regain his composure.*

- Pick up your puppy's paw and immediately click and treat. Repeat this five times and then continue forward by adding an additional one second each time you pick up his paw until ten seconds is reached.

- Hold the paw for ten-twelve seconds with no struggling from your dog. Begin with two seconds then in different sessions work your way to twelve.

- Hold the paw and move it around.

- Massage the paw.

- Pretend to trim the nails.

Side Note: Do not trim your dog's nails unless you are positively sure you know what you are doing. It is not easy and it can cause extreme pain to your dog if you are not properly trained.

The Collar

Find a quiet, low distraction place to practice, grab treats, and put your puppy's collar on him.

- While gently restrained, touch your dog's collar underneath his chin, and then release him right away simultaneously clicking and treating him. Do this about ten times or until your puppy seems comfortable and relaxed with it.

- Grab and hold the collar where it is under his chin and hold it for about 2 seconds, C/T, and repeat. Increase the amount of time until you have achieved about ten seconds of holding and your puppy remains calm. Click and treat after each elapsed amount of time. Work your way up 2,4,6,8 to 10 seconds of holding. This may take several days and sessions.

- Hold the collar under his chin and now give it a little tug. If he accepts this and does not resist, click and treat, and repeat. If he squirms, keep a gentle hold on the collar until he calms down, and then C/T and release him. Repeat this step until he is content with it.

Now, switch to the top of the collar and repeat the whole progression again. Remember slowly increase the time held and the intensity of the tug using a slow pace.

You can pull or tug, but *do not jerk* your puppy's neck or head because this could cause injury and interfere with your outcome objectives of the training exercise. You can practice touching the collar while you are treating during training other tricks. Gently hold the bottom or top of the collar when you are giving your dog a treat reward for successfully completing a commanded behavior.

From the mouth of dog's

- Gently touch your puppy's mouth, *click and treat*, and repeat ten times.

- Touch the side of your puppy's mouth and lift a lip to expose a tooth, *click and treat*, then release only after he stops resisting.

- Gently and slowly, lift the lip to expose more and more teeth on both sides of the mouth, and then open the mouth. Then release when he does not resist, *click and treat*. Be cautious with this one.

- Touch a tooth with a toothbrush, then work up to brushing your puppy's teeth for one to ten-seconds, and then later increase the time. Brushing your puppy's teeth is something you will be doing a few times weekly for the lifetime of your dog.

Do you ear what I ear?

- Reach around the side of your puppy's head, and then briefly and gently touch his ear. Click and treat, repeat ten times.

- When your puppy is comfortable with this, continue and practice holding the ear for one-second. If he is calm, click and treat. If he squirms, stay with him until he is calm. When your puppy calms down, click and treat, then release the ear. Do this until ten seconds is completed with no wiggling.

- Maneuver your pup's ear and pretend that you are cleaning it. Do this gently and slowly so that your puppy learns to enjoy it. It will take a few days of practice until your puppy is calm enough for the real ear cleaning. If your puppy is already sensitive about his ears being touched, it will take longer. See ear cleaning in the Basic Care section.

Proceed slowly at your puppy's comfortable pace. There is no rush, just the end goal of your pup enjoying being handled by you in all sorts of ways that are beneficial to him.

A tell of the tail

Many puppies are sensitive about having their tails handled, and rightly so. Think about if someone grabs you by the arm and you are not fully ready. That is similar to the reaction a puppy feels when grabbed, especially when their tails are handled.

- Start by briefly touching his tail. When moving to touch your puppy's tail move slowly and let your hand be seen moving towards his tail. This keeps your puppy from being startled. Repeat this ten times with clicking and treating, until you notice your puppy is comfortable with his tail being touched.

- Increase the duration of time you hold his tail until you achieve the ten-second mark.

- Tenderly and cautiously, pull the tail up, brush the tail, and then tenderly pull on it until your dog allows you to do this without reacting by jerking, wiggling, or whimpering.

Children, 'nuff said

You must prepare your poor puppy to deal with the strange, unwelcome touching that is often exacted on them by children. Alternatively, you could just put a sign around his neck that says; "You must be at least 16 to touch this puppy." However, it is very likely that your puppy will encounter children that are touchy, grabby, or pokey.

- Prepare your puppy for the strange touches that children may perpetrate. Prepare him by practicing while clicking and treating him for accepting these odd bits of contact such as ear tugs, tail tugs, and perhaps a little harder than usual head pats, kisses, and hugs. Keep in mind, as previously mentioned, puppies and kids are not a natural pairing, *but cheese and wine are*. Even a puppy that is *good with kids* can be pushed to a breaking point and then things can get ugly.

Always supervise children around your dog. ALWAYS! – It is a dog ownership law.

Can you give me a lift?

An emergency may arise that requires you to pick up your dog. As you do these maneuvers, move and proceed slowly and cautiously. First, briefly put your arms around your dog and then give him a click and treat if he stays still. Increase the time duration with successive repetitions. Your dog should be comfortable for ten to fifteen seconds with your arms around him. Next, slowly proceed lifting your dog off the ground and back down, then click and treat when he does not wriggle. Increase the time and the distance you that you lift him from the ground and then move your dog from one place to another. Calculate the time it might take to lift and carry your dog from the house and place him into your vehicle. This is a good time goal to set for carrying your dog.

Eventually, by lifting your dog up and placing him on a table, you will be able to prepare your dog for trips to the groomer, open spaces, or the vet. If you own an extra large dog, or dog that is too heavy for you to lift, solicit help for this training from family or a friend. *Gigantor* may take two to lift safely and properly, or use one of the methods below.

Once up on the table you can practice handling in ways a groomer or veterinarian might handle your dog. This is good preparation for a day at the dog spa or veterinary procedures.

Ways to lift a dog

To lift a large dog properly, always start by approaching the dog from the side. Place one of your hands upon the dog's rear end with the tail in the down position, unless it is a curly tailed spitz type dog that will not enjoy having its tail forced down. This protects the dog's tail from being forced painfully upwards should your arm slip. You should be holding your dog directly underneath the dog's rear hips. Your other hand should be in the front of the dog around his front legs with your arm across his chest. Now your arms should be on your dog's chest and butt area. Then gently press your arms together as in a cradling position and lift using your legs. The human's body position should be that of having bent legs and crouching down so that the power in the legs is used to lift you and your dog upright. To prevent injury to yourself, keep your back as straight as possible.

Small dogs are simpler to lift and require much less effort, but still take great care not to inadvertently injure them. Place your hand in between the back and front legs underneath the dog's underbelly. Supporting the rear with your forearm and placing a hand on the dogs chest is a good idea for extra safety in case your dog squirms when being lifted.

For extra large or dogs that are too heavy for you to lift, purchase and utilize a ramp so that your dog can walk itself into your vehicle. This saves you and your dog from possible or inevitable injury. It is always best to use caution instead of risking a painful, costly, or permanent injury. Of course, you can also teach your dog to jump into the vehicle. Later when your dog becomes aged, you can then utilize the ramp.

Some large dogs can be taught to put their front paws up onto the vehicle floorboard or tailgate, thus allowing you to help push them from their buttocks and assist them jumping in your vehicle.

Never grab, pull, or lift a dog by its fore or rear legs. This can cause serious pain and injury to a dog.

The brush off

- Get your puppy's brush and lightly touch him with it all over his body. If he remains unmoving, give him a click and treat, then repeat. Repeat this until you can brush his whole body and he does not move.

Your puppy will become comfortable with all varieties of touching and handling if you work slowly, patiently, and with plenty of good treats. Handling training is a very important step in your dog's socialization to make him comfortable with being handled.

~ Paws On – Paws Off ~

Basic Care, Dog and Human Goals

Chow Time

- Low Quality Foods: Stay away from corn, wheat, by products, artificial preservatives, and artificial colors. Also, avoid anything in the 'eetos' food group, such as Cheetos, Doritos, burritos, and mosquitoes.

- Avoid junk food, period. It also helps if you do not teach your dog how to use your cell phone and order a pizza. Consult your veterinarian if you think you need specific diet guidance for your dog.

Handling

- Your Dog needs to be comfortable being touched on paws, ears, tail, mouth, entire body, and this should be practiced daily.

Basic Care

Oral maintenance, clipping, and other grooming will depend upon you and your dog's activities. We all know our dogs love to roll and run through all sorts of possible ugly messes, and put obscene things into their mouths, then afterward run up to lick us. Below is a list of the basic grooming care your dog requires. Pick up a grooming book on your specific breed so that you know what and how often your dog needs particular services, extra care areas, and what you may need to have done by professionals.

Most basic care can easily be done at home by you, but if you are unsure or uncomfortable about something, get some tutelage and in no time you will be clipping, trimming, and brushing like a professional.

Coat Brushing - Daily brushing of your dogs coat can be done, or a minimum of 4-5 times a week depending upon your breed's coat. Some breeds blow their coat once or twice a year and daily brushing is recommended during this period. Many breeds do not require daily brushing but it is still healthy for the coat and skin.

Some Equipment: Longhaired dogs need pin brushes, short, medium, and some longhaired dogs need bristle brushes. Slicker brushes remove mats and dead hair. Rubber Curry Combs polish smooth coats. There are clippers, stripping knives, rakes, and more or less are needed, depending upon your dog's coat.

Bathing - Regular but not frequent bathing is essential. Much depends upon your breed's coat. Natural coat oils are needed to keep your dogs coat and skin moisturized. Never bathe your dog too frequently. Depending upon what your dog has been into, a bath once month is adequate. For most breeds, bathing should be done at least once per month, with plenty of warm water and a gentle shampoo or soap made for dogs. Some breeds only require bathing when the odor can no longer be tolerated, so again, read up on your breeds needs.

Nail trimming – For optimal foot health, your dog's nails should be kept short. There are special clippers that are needed for nail trimming that are designed to avoid injury. You can start trimming when your dog is a puppy, and you should have no problems. However, if your dog still runs for the hills or squirms ike an eel at trimming time, then your local groomer or veterinarian can do this procedure.

Ear cleaning – You should clean your dog's ears at least once a month depending upon your breed, but be sure to inspect them every few days for bugs such as mites and ticks. Also, look for any odd discharge, which can be an indication of infection, requiring a visit to the vet. Remember to clean the outer ear only, by using a damp cloth or a cotton swab doused with mineral oil.

Eye cleaning - Use a moist cotton ball to clean any discharge from the eye. Avoid putting anything irritating around, or into your dog's eyes.

Brushing teeth - Pick up a specially designed canine tooth brush and cleaning paste. Clean your dog's teeth as frequently as daily. Try to brush your dog's teeth a few times a week at a minimum. If your dog wants no part of having his or her teeth brushed, try rubbing his teeth and gums with your finger. After he is comfortable with this, you can now put some paste on your finger, allowing him to smell and lick it, then repeat rubbing his teeth and gums with your finger. Now that he is comfortable with your finger, repeat with the brush. In addition, it's important to keep plenty of chews around to promote the oral health of your pooch. When your dog is 2-3 years old, he or she may need their first professional teeth cleaning. Dogs such as Chihuahua's are notorious for having poor teeth and require frequent attention.

Anal sacs - These sacs are located on each side of a dog's anus. If you notice your dog scooting his rear, or frequently licking and biting at his anus, the anal sacs may be impacted. You can ask your veterinarian how to diagnose and treat this issue.

Doing Things: Fun and Educational

- To avoid doggy boredom, make sure you have plenty of toys for your dog to choose from out of the toy bin. A Nylabone™, a Kong™, dog chews, ropes, balls, and tugs are many of the popular things your dog can enjoy. Your more advanced breeds might enjoy mahjong, air hockey, or play station. Please limit their time playing video games.

Be sure your dog is:

- Comfortable with human male and female adults.

- Comfortable with human male and female children.

- Comfortable with special circumstance people, for example, those in wheel chairs, with crutches, braces, or even strange "Uncle Larry."

To assure that your dog isn't selfish, make sure that he or she is:

- Comfortable with sharing his food bowl, toys or bed being touched by you or others.

- Comfortable sharing the immediate space with strangers, especially with children. This is necessary for your puppy's socialization so that he doesn't get paranoid or freak out in small places. For example, elevators in Hollywood filled with celebrities and their handbags, or next-door neighbor's house.

- Comfortable sharing his best friend, YOU, and all family members and friends.

For road trippn' with your dog, make sure he or she is:

- Comfortable in a car, truck, minivan, or in a form of public transportation.

- Always properly restrained.

- Knows how to operate a stick shift as well as an automatic.

In general, a happy puppy should have the following:

- You should provide at least 10 hours of sleep per night for your dog. This should occur in one of the household's adult bedrooms, but not in your bed. He or she should have their own bed or mat available to them.

- Regular health checks at the vet are essential. He or she should receive at least the basic vaccinations, which includes rabies and distemper. Read up before agreeing on extra vaccinations and avoid unnecessary vaccinations or parasite treatments.

- Unless you are going to breed your dog, it is necessary that they be neutered or spayed.

- Maintain a proper weight for your dog. You should be able to feel his ribs but they do not stick out. He or she will have their weight checked at the vet and this will inform you on your dog's optimal weight.

- Plenty of play-time outside with proper supervision.

- It is essential that your dog have daily long walks, play, sport, or games. *~ Paws On – Paws Off ~*

Dog Nutrition

As for nutrition, humans study it, practice it, complain about it, but usually give into the science of it. Like humans, dogs have their own nutrition charts to follow, and are subject to different theories and scientific studies, as well.

In the following, we will look at the history of dog food, as well as the common sense of raw foods, nutrient lists, and what your dog might have to bark about regarding what he is ingesting.

In the beginning, there were wild packs of canines everywhere and they ate anything that they could get their paws on. Similar to human survival, dogs depended upon meat from kills, grasses, berries, and other edibles that nature provided them. Guess what the great news is? Many millennia later nature is still providing all that we need.

Some History

In history, the Romans wrote about feeding their dogs barley bread soaked in milk along with the bones of sheep. The wealthy Europeans of the 1800's would feed their dogs better food than most humans had to eat. Meat from horses and other dead animals was often rounded up from the streets to recycle as dog food for the rich estates on the outskirts of the city. Royalty is legendary for pampering their dogs with all sorts of delicacies from around the world. Meanwhile, the poor and their dogs had to fend for themselves or starve. Being fed table scraps from a pauper's diet was not sufficient to keep a dog healthy, and the humans themselves often had their own nutrition problems. To keep from starving dogs would hunt rats, rabbits, mice, and any other rodent type creature they could sink their teeth.

Other references from the 18th century tell of how the French would mix breadcrumbs with tiny pieces of meat for their dogs. It is also written that the liver, heart, blood, or all, were mixed with milk or cheese and sometimes bread was a manmade food source for domestic canine. In England, they would offer soups flavored with meat and bone to augment their dog's nutrition.

In the mid to late 1800's a middle class blossomed out of the industrial revolution. This group started taking on dogs as house pets and unwittingly created an enterprise out of feeding the household pets that were suddenly in abundance. This new class with its burgeoning wealth had extra money to spend. Noting that the sailor's biscuits kept well for long periods, James Spratt began selling his own recipe of hard biscuit for dogs in London, and shortly thereafter, he took his new product to New York City. It is believed that he single-handedly started the American dog food business. This places the dog food and kibble industry at just over 150 years old, and now is an annual multi-billion dollar business.

All the while we know that any farm dog, or for that matter, any dog that can kill something and eat it will do just that. Nothing has changed throughout the centuries. Raw meat does not kill dogs, so it is safe to say that raw food diets will not either.

Raw Food Stuff

Let us take a look-see at the raw food diet for canines. First, remember that our dogs, pals, best friends, comedy actors, were meant to eat real food such as meat. Their DNA does not only dictate them to eat dry cereals that were concocted by humans in white lab coats. These cereals based and meat-by products may have been keeping our pets alive, but possibly not thriving at optimum levels.

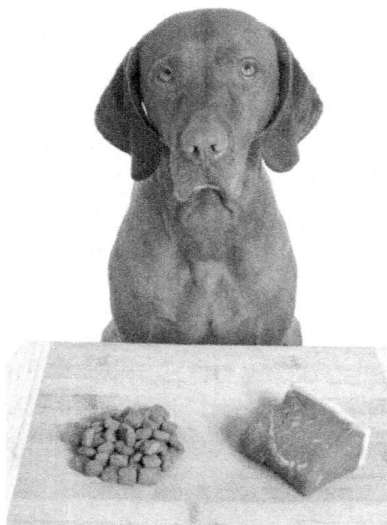

There are many arguments for the benefits of real and raw foods. Sure it is more work, but isn't their health worth it? It is normal, not abnormal to be feeding your dog, a living food diet; it is thought that it will greatly boost their immune system and over-all health. *All foods,* dry, wet, or raw contain a risk, as they can all contain contaminants and parasites.

There are different types of raw food diets. There are raw meats that you can prepare at home by freeze-drying or freezing that you can easily thaw to feed your dog.

Raw food diets amount to foods that are not cooked or sent through a processing plant. With some research, you can make a decision on what you think is the best type of diet for your dog. For your dog's health and for their optimal benefits it is worth the efforts of your research time to read up on a raw foods diet, or possibly a mix of kibble and raw foods.

Rules of thumb to follow for a raw food diet

1. Before switching, make sure your dog has a healthy gastro-intestinal track.

2. Be smart and do not leave meat un-refrigerated for lengthy periods.

3. To be safe, simply follow human protocol for food safety. Toss out the smelly, slimy, or the meat and other food items that just do not seem right.

4. Keep it balanced. Correct amount of vitamins and minerals, fiber, antioxidants, and fatty acids. Note any medical issues your dog has and possible diet correlations.

5. A gradual switch over between foods is recommended to allow their GI track to adjust. Use new foods as a treat, and then watch stools to see how your dog is adjusting.

6. Take note of the size and type of bones you throw to your dog. Not all dogs do well with real raw bones.

7. Freezing meats for three days, similar to sushi protocol, can help kill unwanted pathogens or parasites.

8. Take note about what is working and not working with your dog's food changes. Remember to be vigilant, and take note of your observations when tracking a new diet. If your dog has a healthy issue, your veterinarian will thank you for your thorough note taking.

9. Like us humans, most dogs do well with a variety of foods. There is no one-size-fits-all diet.

10. Please read up on raw foods diet before switching over, and follow all veterinary guidelines.

Human Foods for Dogs

Many human foods are safe for dogs. In reality, human and dog foods were similar for most of our coexistence. Well, maybe we wouldn't eat some of the vermin they eat, but if we were hungry enough we could.

Whether you have your dog on a raw food diet, a partial raw food diet, or manufactured dog foods, you can still treat with some human foods. Even a top quality dog food may be lacking in some nutrients your dog may need. In addition, a tasty safe human food, such as an apple can be used as a treat in training. Below is a short list of some safe human foods that you may feed your dog. Remember to proceed in moderation to see how your dog's digestive system reacts and adjusts to each different food. Always keep plenty of clean fresh drinking water available for your dog.

Short List of SAFE Human Foods for Dogs

Oatmeal

Oatmeal is a fantastic alternative human food source of grain for dogs that are allergic to wheat. Oatmeal's fiber can also be beneficial to more mature dogs. A general set of rules can be followed when feeding your dog oatmeal. Limit the serving sizes, and amount of serving times per week, be sure to serve the oatmeal fully cooked, and finally never add any sugar or additional flavoring.

Apples

REMOVE the seeds. Apples are an excellent human food safe for dogs to crunch on. My dog loves to munch on apples. Apples offer small amounts of both vitamin C and Vitamin A. They are a good source of fiber for a dog of any age. Caution! Do not let your dog eat the seeds of the apple OR the core as they are known to contain minute amounts of cyanide. A few will not be detrimental, so do not freak out if it happens. Just be cautious and avoid the core and seeds when treating.

Brewer's Yeast

This powder has a tangy taste that dogs will clamber over. The yeast is rich in B vitamins, which are great for the dog's skin, nails, ears, and coat. Do not confuse this with 'baking yeast,' which can make your dog ill if eaten. All you need to do is add a couple of sprinkles of brewer's yeast on your dog's food to spice it up. Most dogs really enjoy this stuff.

Brewer's yeast is made from a one-celled fungus called Saccharomyces cerevisiae and is used to make beer. Brewer's yeast is a rich source of minerals, particularly chromium, which is an essential trace mineral that helps the body maintain normal blood sugar levels, selenium, protein, and the B-complex vitamins. Brewer's yeast has been used for years as a nutritional supplement.

Eggs

Does your dog need a protein boost? Eggs are a super supplemental food because they contain ample amounts of protein; selenium, riboflavin, and they are also easily digested by your dog. Cook eggs before serving them to your best buddy, because the cooking process makes more protein available, and it make them more digestible. Eggs are good for energy, strength, and great for training as well.

Green Beans

A lean dog is a happier, more energetic dog. Feeding your dog, cooked green beans is a good source of manganese, and the vitamins C and K, additionally is they are considered a good source of fiber. If you have a lazier dog, living *"A Dog's Life,"* then it is good to be proactive with your dog's weight. Add a steady stream of fresh green beans in your dog's diet for all the right reasons. Avoid salt.

Sweet Potatoes

Vitamin C, B-6, manganese, beta-carotene, and fiber can be found in sweet potatoes. Slice them up and dehydrate and you have just found a great new healthy source for treating your dog. Next time you are out shopping for potatoes, pick up sweet potatoes, and see if your best little buddy takes to them. My bet is that your dog will love them.

Pumpkins

Pumpkins are a fantastic source of vitamin A, fiber, and beta-carotene. Trend towards a healthy diet with plenty of fiber and all the essential vitamins and proteins your dog needs. Pumpkin is one way to help you mix it up a bit. Feed it dried or moist, separate as a treat, or with his favorite foods. Pumpkin can be a fantastic, fun, and natural alternative food for dogs.

Salmon

A great source of omega 3 fatty acids, salmon is an excellent food that can support your dog's immune system, as well as his skin, coat, and overall health. Some dog owners notice when adding salmon to their dog's diet that it increases resistance to allergies. Be sure to cook the salmon before serving it. You can use salmon oil too. For treats, added flavoring to a meal, or as a complete meal, salmon is a fantastic source of natural, real food that is safe for dogs.

Flax Seed

Grounded or in oil form, flax seed is a nourishing source of omega 3 fatty acids. Omega 3 fatty acids are essential in helping your dog maintain good skin and a shiny healthy coat. Note; you will want to serve the flax seed directly after grinding it because this type of fatty acid can turn sour soon after. Flax seed is also a wonderful source of fiber your dog or puppy needs.

Yogurt

Always a great source for your dog's calcium and protein, yogurt is another one of our top ten human foods safe for dogs. Pick a fat free yogurt with no added sweeteners, or artificial sugar, color, or flavoring.

Melons

Additionally, watermelons, cantaloupes, honeydews are good for your dog. Without prior research, avoid any exotic melons or fruits.

Peanut butter

Yep, a big spoon full and it will keep him occupied for a while.

Berries (fresh & frozen)

Blueberries, blackberries, strawberries, huckleberries or raspberries provide an easy and tasty snack.

Cooked chicken

Chicken sliced up is a favorite yummy snack for your canine to enjoy in addition, or in place of his regular meal.

Beef and Beef Jerky

Jerky is a great high-value treating item for training, and beef is can be a healthy addition to your dog's diet.

Cheese

Sliced or cubed pieces are great for training or in the place of food. A tablespoon of cottage cheese on top of your dog's food will certainly be a healthy hit. Try using string cheese as a training treat.

Bananas

All fruits have phytonutrients, and other required nutrients that are essential to your canine's health.

Carrots

Crunchy veggies are good for the teeth. Carrots are full of fiber and vitamin A.

UNSAFE Human Foods

Below is a list of harmful foods for dogs. This is not a complete list, but a common list of foods known to be harmful to our canine friends. If you are unsure of a food that you wish to add to your dog's diet, please consult a veterinarian or expert on dog nutrition.

Onions: Both onions and garlic contain the toxic ingredient thiosulphate. However, onions are more dangerous than garlic because of this toxin. Many dog biscuits contain *trace* amounts of garlic, and because of this small amount, there is no threat to the health of your dog. This poison can be toxic in one large dose, or with repeated consumption that builds to the toxic level in the dog's blood.

Chocolate: Contains theobromine, a compound that is a cardiac stimulant and a diuretic. This can be fatal to dogs.

Grapes: Contains an unknown toxin that can affect kidney, and in large enough amounts can cause acute kidney failure.

Raisins: (Same as above)

Most Fruit Pits and Seeds: Contains cyanogenic glycosides, which if consumed can cause cyanide poisoning. The fruits by themselves are okay to consume.

Macadamia Nuts: Contains an unknown toxin that can be fatal to dogs.

Most Bones: Should not be given (especially chicken bones) because they can splinter and cause a laceration of the digestive system or pose a choking hazard because of the possibility for them to become lodged in your pet's throat.

Potato Peelings and Green Potatoes: Contains oxalates, which can affect the digestive, nervous, and urinary systems.

Rhubarb leaves: Contains high amount of oxalates.

Broccoli: Broccoli should be avoided, though it is only dangerous in large amounts.

Green parts of tomatoes: Contains oxalates, which can affect the digestive, nervous, and urinary systems.

Yeast dough: Can produce gas and swell in your pet's stomach and intestines, possibly leading to a rupture of the digestive system.

Coffee and tea: (due to the caffeine)

Alcoholic Beverages: Alcohol is very toxic to dogs and can lead to coma or even death.

Human Vitamins: Vitamins containing iron are especially dangerous. These vitamins can cause damage to the lining of the digestive system, the kidneys, and liver.

Moldy or spoiled foods: There are many possible harmful outcomes from spoiled foods.

Persimmons: These can cause intestinal blockage.

Raw Eggs: Salmonella.

Salt: In large doses can cause an electrolyte imbalance.

Mushrooms: Can cause liver and kidney damage.

Avocados: Avocado leaves; fruit, seeds, and bark contain a toxin known as persin. The Guatemalan variety that is commonly found in stores appears to be the most problematic. Avocados are known to cause respiratory distress in other animals, but causes less harmful problems in dogs. It is best to avoid feeding them to your dog.

Xylitol: This artificial sweetener is not healthy for dogs.

According to nutritional scientists and veterinarian health professionals, your dog needs twenty Amino Acids, and ten of which are essential. At least thirty-six nutrients and a couple of extra may be needed to combat certain afflictions. Your dog's health depends upon the intake of the following nutrients. Read labels and literature to take stock of the foods you provide.

36 Nutrients for dogs:

1. 10 essential Amino Acids – Arginine, Histidine, Isoleucine, Leucine, Lysine, Methionine. Along with Phenylalanine, Threonine, Tryptophan, and Valine.

2. 11 vitamins – A, D, E, B1, B3, B5, B6, B12, Folic Acid, and Choline.

3. 12 minerals – Calcium, Phosphorus, Potassium, Sodium, Chloride, Magnesium, Copper, Manganese, Zinc, Iodine, and Selenium

4. Fat – Linoleic Acid

5. Omega 6 Fatty Acid

6. Protein

Suggested Daily Quantities of Recommended Nutrients		
Nutritient	**Puppies**	**Adult Dogs**
Protein (%)	22.0	18.0
Arginine (%)	0.62	0.51
Histidine (%)	0.22	0.18
Isoleucine (%)	0.45	0.37
Leucine (%)	0.72	0.59
Lysine (%)	0.77	0.63
Methionine + cystine (%)	0.53	0.43
Phenylalanine + tyrosine (%)	0.89	0.73
Threonine (%)	0.58	0.48
Tryptophan (%)	0.20	0.16
Valine (%)	0.48	0.39
Fat (%)	8.0	5.0
Calcium (%)	1.0	0.6
Phosphorus (%)	0.8	0.5
Sodium (%)	0.3	0.06
Chloride (%)	0.45	0.09

We realize it may take time to understand what kind of diet your dog will thrive. Do your best to include in your dogs daily diet, all thirty-six nutrients mentioned here. All of which can come from fruits, veggies, kibble, raw foods, and yes, even good table scraps. You will soon discover that your dog has preferred foods. For your dog to maintain optimum health, he needs a daily basis of a GI track healthy, well-rounded diet with a good balance of exercise, rest, socializing, care, and love.

~ Paws On – Paws Off ~

That's All Folks

Believe me, this is not everything that there is to know about dogs. Training your Bearded Collie is a lifelong endeavor. There are a myriad of other methods, tricks, tools, and things to teach and learn with your dog. You are never finished, but this is half of the fun of having a dog, as he or she is a constant work in progress. Your dog is living art.

If your training experience is anything similar to mine, there were days and times when you thought your dog would never catch on, or seemed interested in participating and learning. I hope that you were able to work through the difficult times and the result is that you and your dog now understand one another at a high level, and that you are in command of your dog.

Owning and befriending our dogs is a lifetime adventurous commitment that is worthwhile and rewarding on every level. It seems as though many times Axel knows what I am thinking and acts or reacts accordingly, but he and I are together more than most of my family members. Through the good and bad times, he always makes me smile, sometimes when he is being the orneriest I smile the biggest. He is such a foolhardy, loveable, intelligent, and clownish dog, how could anyone be sad around him.

Remember, it is important to learn to think like your dog. Patience with your dog, as well as with yourself is vital. If you do this right, you will have a relationship and a bond that will last for years. The companionship of a dog can bring joy and friendship like none other. Keep this book handy and reference it often. In addition, look for other resources, such as training books, and utilizing like-minded experienced friends with dogs that can share their successes and failures. Never stop broadening your training skills. Your efforts will serve to keep you and your Bearded Collie happy and healthy for a long, long time.

Thanks for reading! I hope that you enjoyed this as much as I have enjoyed writing it. If this training guide informed how to train your dog, please comment in Amazon and tell others about the positive information in this guide. Please use the Amazon comment format of listing both the pro-con that you found when reading and implementing this training guide. I am always striving to improve both my writing and training skills. I look forward to reading your comments.

~ Paws On – Paws Off ~

"A Big 'Barking' Thank You!"

Did you know that underneath my shaggy brown hair there are two gigantic ears and that they are great for listening too? Can you please help me put these enormous, floppy radar dishes into good use, and tell me if I helped you to **train your dog**? **Can You Train Your Dog Now?**

You Can Tell Me with a *Quick and* <u>Positive Review Here</u>

*Or... you can read even more of my **begging for glory** below. (Yawn)*

Why Write a Review Today?

Well, it has to do with the *'Law of Diminishing Intent'.- Huh?* In essence, this means that the more anyone waits to complete an action, the more our reasons become cloudy, and soon not important enough to act out.

The truth is, I want to be the best, but I would be foolish to assume I could become the best alone, so I am asking you for your feedback.

This is Where you Can Help Me, Help More!

Just write a short, quick review, telling other new dog owners how charming I am, ahem, and if now you know **How to Train Your Dog!**

It is Super Simple Too! *<u>Just Answer One Single Question.</u>*

144

Did you learn How to Train Your Dog?

Answer: *"YES because…"* [This probably means 5-Stars Right?]
Answer: *"YES, but…"* [Again 5-Stars, but also add your suggestions!]

Do you **HAVE** to give me a 5-Star Review? Nope, you can go super negative, humiliate me, my kids, my dogs, and if it puts more meat on your bone, rip out my mailbox. However, no one **WINS** if you do.

Best Way: Go bigger, stay positive, and help me to help others.

Make Me Proud - Be Loud in *that* Cloud: - REVIEW ME HERE https://www.amazon.com/dp/B00JF5VHUI

- Thank you very much for all of your help in helping me, and others! – Paul

DON'T THiNK — BE, ALPHA DOG

I wrote this book to inform and instruct dog owners of the fundamentals for establishing and maintaining the *alpha* position within the household hierarchy. Inside the book you will learn how to live, lead, train, and love your dog in a **non-physical alpha dog way**. Leading from the *alpha* position makes everything dog related *easier*. All dogs need to know where they are positioned within the family (pack), and to understand, and trust that their *alpha* will provide food, shelter, guidance, and affection towards them. Then life becomes *easier* for you and your dog

Whether or not you have read one of my "Think Like a dog..." breed specific training books, I am confident that this guide will assist you while you train your dog companion. With these *alpha* fundamentals, your dog will obey your commands in critical situations, and follow your lead into a safer and happier life. Remember, having an obedient dog keeps other animals and humans safe.

A dog that respects his *alpha* leader is easier to control, teach, and trust. He is more likely to obey your commands and respect your rules. Be the *alpha* now.

~ Paps

"Alpha Dog Secrets" by Paul Allen Pearce

LEARN MORE:

http://www.amazon.com/dp/B00ICGQO40

Hey...Did I miss something?

STUMPED?

Got a Question about Your Bearded Collie?

Ask an Expert Now!

Facebook ~

https://www.facebook.com/newdogtimes

NewDogTimes ~

http://newdogtimes.com/

It's where the **Bearded Collie Secrets** *have been hidden - since their Ancestral Wolf Packs were forced to collide with Man...*

Wait Until You Learn This

BONUS TRICKS
Teaching the "Touch" Command

Excerpted from the book "49 ½ Dog Tricks"

By Paul Allen Pearce

Available in 2015

Introduction

Did you ever want to amaze and entertain your friends and family with the type of dog that can, will, and wants to do anything at anytime, a show-off dog? You know that dog that understands vocal and body signals, reacts when commanded, and is a great companion in life. The tricks inside this book are the kind of fun and useful tricks that can give you that kind of dog when together you master them. After training these tricks included inside this book, you and your dog can have a joyful and fruitful life together as friends and partners in showmanship.

Trick #10 Teaching "Touch"

Touch has an easy rating and requires no knowledge of other tricks, but your dog should know its name. The supplies needed are a wooden dowel to be used as a touch stick, your clicker, and some treats.

Touch training teaches your dog to touch, and in this lesson to touch the end of a stick. It can be any type of wooden dowel, cut broom handle, or similar that is around three feet (.9 meters) in length. During training, add a plastic cap, rubber ball, or good ole duct tape to the end so that there are no sharp edges that can harm your dog. A good sanding will also cure the problem of rough or sharp edges.

Teaching "touch" using the *touch stick* will enable you to train other tricks. You will discover that the *touch stick* is useful in training, so take care that you correctly train your dog the *touch* command. **Touch is used later to teach Learn Names, Ring Bell, Jump Over People, Spin, Jump, and more.**

1. To begin, have your dog in the sitting position or standing near you and giving his attention towards you. Hold your stick away from your body. Keep holding it while doing nothing else but holding the stick steady at a level that your dog can easily touch it with his nose.

2. Luckily, dog's natural curiosity will get the best of them and your dog should touch the stick. When your dog touches it with his nose or mouth, *click and treat*. Be sure to click immediately when your dog touches the end of the stick. Sometimes it is just a sniff, but those count for beginning to shape the command.

If your dog is not interested then you will need to do the touching for him. Do this by gently touching your dog's nose while simultaneously clicking and then treating. Keep doing this until your dog is regularly touching the stick when you hold it out.

3. The next time your dog touches the stick C/T while simultaneously saying the command, "touch." Remember timing is important in all tricks. Your dog needs to know the exact action that is the correct action, which he is being rewarded for performing. Repeat this a dozen times. Continue over multiple sessions until your dog upon command of "touch," is easily touching the end of the touch stick. Feel free to add some "good dog" praises.

Hands On

Teaching Jake this trick was an interesting outing. When I first held out the stick, Jake swiped it away with his paw. After a couple of more times, he finally smelled the end with his nose and I quickly clicked and treated. He responded quickly to that, and after reinforcing that with several more *click and treats*, he started quickly touching the end of the stick.

After using the *touch* command a dozen times, he realized a treat came after he touched the end of the stick, and moving forward through a few training sessions, he started touching it each time I issued my "touch" command. I kept practicing and after a couple of more sessions, I locked it in with Jake. I was then able to use the "touch" command and touch stick to train other tricks.

If your dog is coming in hard to touch the stick, you can add some foam to the end of the stick to cushion his *super-nose*.

Troubleshooting

What if my dog is touching the middle of the stick, or not touching the stick at all?

I mentioned that Jake took a few swipes at the end of the stick before touching it. Each time he did this, I ignored this behavior even though he looked at me expecting a reward. He could smell the treats in my hand, but I did not click and reward the wrong action. Finally, as I held the stick out close to his snout, he smelled it with his nose and I quickly clicked and treated.

Do not reward until your dog is touching *only* the end of the stick. This allows you to use the touch command in training other tricks. If your dog will not touch it try gently touching the end of the stick to his nose and C/T, but quickly move away from that and let your dog begin to do the touching on his own.

"49 ½ Dog Tricks"

By Paul Allen Pearce

Will be available in 2015

Teaching to Learn Names

Excerpted from the book "49 ½ Dog Tricks"

By Paul Allen Pearce

Available in 2015

Trick #15 - Learn Names

Learning names has an intermediate to difficult rating and requires knowledge of the touch command. The supplies needed are a toy, treats, and your clicker.

Dog owners have known for years that dogs are smarter than many people give them credit. They are capable of learning the names of many different objects such as their toys, people, and places such as rooms. Using the steps in this exercise your dog can learn the names of all your family members, his personal items such as his crate, collar, and leash. Beyond those items, your dog can learn the names of different rooms, which enable you to use the "go" command to have your dog, go to a specific room. Dogs have been known to learn hundreds and even upwards to a thousand words. Furthermore, once your dog learns the name of something, he or she can find it, take it, and bring it to you.

Not all dogs are capable of learning the same number of words and some will learn and retain better than others, so do not get frustrated if it takes some time for your dog to recognize and remember what object, place, or person goes with the name you are speaking. Select a toy that you may already refer to by name. Chances are that you already often speak the names of dog-associated items when speaking to your dog and he recognizes that word.

Be consistent in your name references to your dog's toys such as Frisbee™, tug, ball, rope, and squeaky.

1. To begin, find a low distraction area, treats at the ready, and one of your dog's favorite toys. I will use *tug* in this example.

2. Start by using *touch* and have your dog touch your empty hand, when he does, *click and treat* your dog. Repeat this five times.

3. Next, grab your dog's toy into your hand, say, "touch," and if he touches the tug and not your hand, C/T your dog.

4. Repeat number three, but this time, add the toy name, say, "touch tug." When your dog touches the *tug*, and nothing else, C/T at that exact moment he does this. Repeat this 6-10 times.

5. After a break, practice steps 1-4 over a few sessions, and a day or two.

6. In the next phase warm up with numbers 1-4, then hold the tug out away from you and say "touch tug," when he does C/T. Repeat this 6-10 times. Then extend the tug at full arm lengths from you and repeat 6-10 times. Practice this over a couple of sessions. Take note of your dogs progress and when he is ready, proceed to number seven.

7. Now, place the tug onto the floor but keep your hand on it, and say, "touch tug," when he does, C/T. Repeat 6-10 times.

8. Now, place it on the floor without your hand upon it, and say, "touch tug," and when he does, treat a barnbuster sized treat serving. Feel free to throw in some verbal good boy/girls. If your dog is not moving to it, be patient, silent, and still, and see if he can figure it out on his own. Remember that your dog wants his treat.

9. Moving forward with the same toy, place it around the room in different areas, increasingly further from you. Place it on top of a small stool, on the ground, and or low-lying shelves and have your dog "touch tug." Practice this over a few days and when your dog is regularly responding move onto number ten and a new toy.

10. Move onto another toy. Use a toy such as Frisbee™ that when said sounds much different when the word is spoken than the previous toy name. Repeat the steps 4-9 with this next toy.

11. Time to test if your dog can tell the difference. Sit down on the couch or floor and place both the Frisbee™ and the tug behind you. Take out the Frisbee and practice five touches, C/T each time your dog correctly touches upon command. Next, do the same with the tug.

12. Now, hold one toy in each hand and say, "touch Frisbee™" and see if your dog touches the correct toy. If your dog touches the Frisbee™, C/T, and give a barnbuster sized reward. If your dog begins to move towards the Frisbee™, but you see that he is unsure, C/T him for moving in the correct direction. If your dog goes to the tug or does nothing, remain neutral offering no C/T or verbal reward.

Keep working on this and practicing until your dog regularly goes to the correct toy that you command to be touched. Then following the same process continue adding toys. When you get to three then four, toys/objects you can lay out all four in front of you and command "touch (object name)" and see if your dog can choose and recognize the correct toy/object.

13. Practice the "touch tug, ball, Frisbee, chew" by placing the objects in different parts of the room and have him identify each correctly. Practice this often to keep the names fresh in your dog's mind.

14. Teaching names of people is done a little differently, because for obvious reasons you cannot hold them in your hand, if they are willing, you could however have them sit on the floor. Trick #8 "Train Your Dog to Go To a Place" will teach you how to use the training stick to help train the names of rooms and things such as crate, bed, and mat. You can use the training stick to introduce the person.

Alternative to #14 - Teaching a person's name to your dog can be taught like this.

1. Hold onto your dog's collar and have a family member show your dog a treat. Have the person walk into the other room. Then say, "Jake, find Michelle," or whatever the person's name is. Now let go of the collar and see if your dog will go into the other room and to that person. It is okay to follow your dog. If he does go to the person, give your dog a C/T and a huge barnbuster reward along with praise.

2. Repeat five times and take a break.

3. After number two, have the family member go into different rooms, and do five repetitions in each room.

4. It will take a few sessions for your dog to learn and retain the names. Do not forget to reinforce practicing forever.

Hands On

I taught this to Jake, but my wife's Poodle Roxie knows many more names of objects, people, and places, but Jake can respectably perform all of the tricks in here. He is my pal and goes through all of these things willingly, but some days I have to give him a break, probably like crash test dummies in the car industry need a break.

Teaching Jake names while using the "touch" command I started out by using the touch command with my empty hand, and getting a peculiar look from him. He touched my hand and I C/T about a half dozen times. Holding Jakes attention while in the sitting position in front of me, I then I picked up the tug into my hand and repeated the exercise saying, "touch tug," and only C/T when he touched the tug. I'll confess it took a few attempts and me adjusting my hand so that he had to touch the tug when he moved his nose towards my hand holding the tug. I ran through exercises 1-4 over a few days and about six sessions.

Eventually, I felt confident to start moving the tug further from my body and then onto the floor, couch cushion, into the corner of the room and so forth. It took some time and patience for him to begin to understand right away to go to the item being named. Eventually, I was able to place it into different rooms inside the house and call out "touch tug" and he would bolt off looking for it. From there I added further toys such as Frisbee™, which I discovered by his ears and the way that he looked at me when I said the word that he already recognized the sound of the word.

Troubleshooting

I am scratching my head because my dog does not understand what I am trying to teach!

In the beginning, you can try maneuvering your hand so that your dog will touch the toy and not your hand.

Watch your time when training. Keep your sessions short and if your dog is still a puppy or acting like one keep your sessions around 3-5 minutes, while older dogs can go about 10 minutes per training session. If you notice any signs of fatigue, end the session on a high, happy note, and stop for the day and begin anew the following day.

Hint: After your dog recognizes, and is regularly touching objects in different locations, solicit other people to practice giving your dog the command. Combine this with "take it" & "bring it" and your dog will go find and bring to you anything he has learned the name. Have fun and enjoy adding objects and names.

...This book contains fun tricks as well as other useful tricks that all dogs should know that would benefit them and their owners. When your dog learns and masters all 49 ½ tricks, you will have a well-mannered, obedient, talented dog that is your friend, show-off, and companion. You two will be sure to get plenty of laughs and applause by combining these fun tricks and utilitarian commands.

I wrote this to help dog owners and trainers further their dog's abilities and the bond between dog and owner...

"49 ½ Dog Tricks"
By Paul Allen Pearce
Will be available in 2015

VISIT US TODAY!

Share Our Links — Like us, Pin us, Feed it, Tweet it and Twerk it — We Need Help Too!

Please Comment "Let us know what you think..., did this book help you with training your dog, please comment on Amazon and write me on Facebook. I am always trying to improve and update my books."

Facebook ~

https://www.facebook.com/newdogtimes

NewDogTimes ~

http://newdogtimes.com

"Thanks for reading. I hope you enjoyed this as much as I have enjoyed writing it and training my dog!"

"Keep on training and loving your Now Zen Like 'Kung-Fu' dog. Please be patient, loving, and have fun while training your dog."

~ Paul Allen Pearce

Think Like a Dog - but Don't Eat Your Poop!

LEARN MORE:

http://www.amazon.com/dp/B00ICGQO40

Bearded Collie Facts

Country of Origin: Scotland

Other Names: Highland Collie, Mountain Collie, Hairy Mou'ed Collie, Argle Bargle

Nicknames: Beardie

Group: Herding, Working, and Pastoral

Size: Large

Height: 53-56cm (20-22in)

Weight: 18-27kg (40-60lbs)

Lifespan: 12-14

Litter: 4-12, Average 7

Colors: Black, blue, brown, or fawn with white and tan markings

Coat: They have a long double coat that requires daily brushing to keep tangles and mats away. Eyes, ears, and paws should be regularly inspected.

Shedding: Average

Apartment: No, and does not like being confined or kenneled.

Temperament: Affectionate, playful, lively, cheerful, and easy going.

Exercise: Daily rigorous exercise through long brisk walks and running free in safe open spaces.

Training: Beardies require a strong leader/trainer, like most herders, they are intelligent and independent.

Notes: Thick coat requires diligent attention and inspection for ticks, burrs and any other critter finding a home inside their thick undercoat. Beardies prefer to be outdoors and their thick coats allow them to tackle all weather conditions. Can be prone to excessive barking but are not guard dogs, but make good watchdogs.

Beardie Rescue

Bearded Collies are often acquired without any clear understanding of what goes into owning one, and these dogs regularly end up in the care of rescue groups, and are badly in need of adoption or fostering. If you are interested in adopting a Beardie, a rescue group is a good place to start. I have listed a few below. If you have the facilities and ability please rescue a dog and enjoy the rewarding experience that it offers both of you.

http://www.animalshelter.org/shelters/states.asp

http://beardedcollieclub.us/rescue/

http://www.beardedcollieclub.co.uk/rescue.php

About the Author

Paul Allen Pearce is the author of many breed specific "Think Like a Dog" & "Think Like Me" dog-training books, "Alpha Dog Secrets Revealed," and others. When his family duties allow, he spends his spare time outdoors with his two dogs Buck and Samson. He lives in the South Eastern part of the United States where he continues his education and writing.

Other Books

"Don't Think BE Alpha Dog Secrets Revealed"

"Think Like a Dog...but don't eat your poop!"
(Breed specific dog training series)

"Think Like Me...but don't eat your poop!
(Breed specific dog training series)

Contributing Editors | Content Attributions

Photos: We wish to thank all of the photographers for sharing their photographs via Creative Commons Licensing.

Flickr - Wiki commons

Link to photo, CC License,name of photo, author, changes made

COVER

http://commons.wikimedia.org/wiki/File:Bearded_Collie_portra it.jpg, By John Haslam (Flickr) [CC BY 2.0 (http://creativecommons.org/licenses/by/2.0)], via Wikimedia Commons

BIO BEARDIE RUNNING

https://www.flickr.com/photos/ariander/4072944194, CC License 2.0 NoDerivs https://creativecommons.org/licenses/by-nd/2.0/legalcode, Beardies-3, By Arild Anderson, no changes

THINGS THAT WORK WHILE TRAINING

http://upload.wikimedia.org/wikipedia/commons/9/90/Buberle .JPG, By UniqueAndreas (Own work (own camera)) [Public domain], via Wikimedia Commons

CLICKER

https://www.flickr.com/photos/56705607@N00/3060081187, CC License 2.0 Generic https://creativecommons.org/licenses/by/2.0/legalcode, IMG_2514, By Blake Handley, no changes

NAME https://www.flickr.com/photos/johnnyh/8646024371, CC License 2.0 Generic https://creativecommons.org/licenses/by/2.0/legalcode, Meet Huggy Bear, By Johnny Hodgson, slight cropping

COME https://www.flickr.com/photos/genewolf/161895019, CC License 2.0 NoDerivs https://creativecommons.org/licenses/by-nd/2.0/legalcode, The Girls, andreavallejos, slight cropping

LEAVE IT

https://www.flickr.com/photos/56705607@N00/7206699536, CC License 2.0 Generic https://creativecommons.org/licenses/by/2.0/legalcode, 2015 05 May 15 01, By Blake Handley, slight color correction

License 2.0 Generic
https://creativecommons.org/licenses/by/2.0/legalcode, Bern
Dog on Leash signs, Andrew Nash, no changes made
Jumping
https://www.flickr.com/photos/emeryway/3109438368, CC
License 2.0 Generic
https://creativecommons.org/licenses/by/2.0/legalcode, Jack
Russell jumping, By Emery
Way
Housetraining -
Lift - https://www.flickr.com/photos/anglerp/457343784/ , CC
License 2.0 https://creativecommons.org/licenses/by-
sa/2.0/legalcode, Anna mini Schnauzer, By Patti, No changes
were made.
Treats -
http://upload.wikimedia.org/wikipedia/commons/e/ef/Treats-
IMGP9845-1.jpg,By Stacy Lynn Baum (Stacy Lynn Baum) [CC-BY-
3.0 (http://creativecommons.org/licenses/by/3.0)], via
Wikimedia Commons, No changes were made
Digger in action -
https://www.flickr.com/photos/31064702@N05/3447086205/,
CC License 2.0 https://creativecommons.org/licenses/by-
sa/2.0/legalcode, taking a break, By Dawn Huczek, No changes
made.
Digging Jack Russell -
https://www.flickr.com/photos/ssicore/428501528, CC License
2.0, gophering, By Stephanie Sicore, No changes were made.
Body Language, Dog by dirt pile -
https://www.flickr.com/photos/31064702@N05/3447086205/,
CC License 2.0 https://creativecommons.org/licenses/by-
sa/2.0/legalcode, taking a break, By Dawn Huczek, No changes
were made.
Basic Care & Human Goals Ear Cleaning
https://www.flickr.com/photos/dogfoto/9108187542, CC
License 2.0
https://creativecommons.org/licenses/by/2.0/legalcode, Lotus,
American_Staffordshire_Terrier, By Jay Lee, No changes made

Photo Attribution Herding Traits

Legal Disclaimer:

The author of **"Think Like a Dog...but don't eat your poop! books,** Paul Allen Pearce is in no way responsible at any time for the action of your pet, not now or in the future. Animals, without warning, may cause injury to humans and/or other animals. Paul Allen Pearce is not responsible for attacks, bites, mauling, nor any other viciousness or any and all other damages. We strongly recommend that you exercise caution for the safety of self, the animal, and all around the animals while working with your dog. We are not liable for any animal or human medical conditions or results obtained from training. While all attempts have been made to verify information provided in this publication, neither the author nor the publisher assume any responsibility for errors, omissions or contrary interpretation of the subject matter contained herein. The publisher and author assume no responsibility or liability whatsoever on the behalf of any purchaser or reader of the material provided. The owner of said dog training guide assumes any and all risks associated with the methodology described inside the dog-training guidebook.

Printed in Great Britain
by Amazon

11274876R00108